A MANUAL FOR MEN
MENTORING MEN

Pastoral Care through Male Mentoring for the
African American Man

JEROME STEVENSON

WESTBOW°
PRESS
A DIVISION OF THOMAS NELSON
& ZONDERVAN

WestBow Press books may be ordered through booksellers or by contacting:

WestBow Press
A Division of Thomas Nelson
1663 Liberty Drive
Bloomington, IN 47403
www.westbowpress.com
1 (866) 928-1240

ISBN: 978-1-4908-1837-5 (sc)

Library of Congress Control Number: 2013922041

Printed in the United States of America.

WestBow Press rev. date: 12/20/2013

The Prologue

The writing of this manual as a book is a result of a conversation with one of my seminary students, Alverta Boozer. She was certain that this manual could be useful to address the issues impacting African American males throughout our communities in America. Our conversation led me to revisit my time in Detroit, Michigan where I had begun to offer workshops on mentoring to local congregations and their pastors. The results were very encouraging as we saw men mentoring men and men mentoring boys throughout metropolitan Detroit.

It is my hope and dream that the work can be expanded as a result of this publishing project. I pray that the Lord will use it to confront the many issues that plague our communities so that there are more of our males in jails than there are in higher education. I pray that the issue of incarceration and lower employment can be impacted by the godly principle taught from the Scriptures.

If this book can be used to change one life, then my living will not have been in vain!!!

Abstract

This model develops a mentoring manual for men in a spiritual Baptist Church of Detroit and its Westside Community.

This mentoring model is not different from discipleship models from a biblical perspective, but it is different in its practical application. Mentoring focuses on relationships and relationship building. Those engaged in discipleship training generally focus on academic models. This model will attempt to make some distinctions between the two models as they are applied in the contemporary church.

Acknowledgments

I am deeply indebted to several people who are responsible for assisting and supporting me with this book. I am very thankful for godly parents. Jimmie and Dorothy Stevenson who gave me a great start in life by raising me in a godly home where I was loved and nurtured. I am very grateful for my wife, Ida, who has always supported me and given me encouragement to pursue my goals and dreams. I acknowledge and appreciate my children Melissa Ruth, Jerome Jr., and Julia who have been great supporters and constant encouragement to me. I owe a debt of gratitude to my pastor, Dr. Samuel Bullock Jr., for trusting me to train the men of the church during this doctoral process. Finally, I owe many thanks to my daughter, Julia Patrice Stevenson for editing, proofreading, advising and supporting me through this process. Above all, I thank God for his blessings that allowed me to endure.

Contents

Chapter 1: Introduction and Rationale 1

Chapter 2: Biblical, Theological, and Historical Foundations. 16

Chapter 3: Review of the Literature 28

Chapter 4: Methods, Procedures, and Research Design 62

Chapter 5: Results 69

Introduction 71

Objectives 72

Pretest 73

Session One.. 79
    Lesson one (week one) 79
    Lesson two (week two) 82
    Lesson three (week three).. 86
    Lesson four (week four) 89
    Lesson five (week five) 95

Session Two 98
    Lesson one (week one) 98
    Lesson two (week two) 101
    Lesson three (week three).. 103
    Lesson four (week four) 106
    Lesson five (week five) 109

Session Three... 117
    Lesson one (week one) 117
    Lesson two (week two) 120
    Lesson three (week three).. 123
    Lesson four (week four) 126
    Lesson five (week five) 129

Session Four 132
  Lesson one (week one) 132
  Lesson two (week two) 139
  Lesson three (week three) 141
  Lesson four (week four) 143
  Lesson five (week five) 145

Session Five 148
  Lesson one (week one) 148
  Lesson two (week two) 151
  Lesson three (week three) 154
  Lesson four (week four) 156
  Lesson five (week five) 158

Appendix One 159

Appendix Two 160

Appendix Three.. 162

Selected Bibliography 163

Chapter 6: Summary and Reflections 166

Appendix One 179

Appendix Two 187

Appendix Three.. 189

Appendix Four.. 191

Appendix Five.. 196

Appendix Six 197

Appendix Seven 214

The Epilogue 217

Selected Bibliography 219

CHAPTER I

Introduction and Rationale

The purpose of this project is to develop a mentoring manual that equips African American men to mentor other African American men.

Overview

The church has a historical role in the life of African American men: it was a place where they could exercise authority, educate themselves and their children, practice entrepreneurship, seek employment, and engage in politics. Considering these significant historical contributions, the lack of male membership in present day churches is disturbing and discouraging. However, this absence is so common among congregations that it has seemingly become the acceptable norm. With this in mind, what now can be done about the decline of male attendance and participation in the church?

This is the development of a mentoring manual targeting directed at African American men. The purpose of the manual is to focus on African American men in an intentional, personal, and relational approach that will lead to a positive change in behavior towards the church and within the community.

Rationale

This book is written in response to a dilemma observed by the writer who is a member of American Baptist Churches. This dilemma is one of social, biblical, theological, and historical significance. The dilemma refers to the significant disproportion of African American males not in attendance of church compared to women and children.

The writer, from observations and discussions with urban African American pastors, has concluded that the increase in active participation and attendance of African American men will also lead to advancing social opportunities. Such opportunities include the strengthening of the African American church, strengthening of African American families, and the renewal of communities. The increase in attendance and participation, on the part of African American males, also leads to positive economic and social implications.

The historical relevance of this project can be found in the many historical events that have influenced African American life. Slavery in America, systemic racism, and discrimination has collectively affected the participation and church attendance of African American men.

One way in which slavery affected the participation of African American men is through the practices introduced in a letter written by Willie Lynch. Although this letter has not been authenticated and may not exist, the concept of helplessness has penetrated through generations of African American males. [1]

Willie Lynch, a slave owner in the West Indies in 1717, identifies strategies to be used by White slave owners in America for controlling the slaves:

> I have outlined a number of differences among the slaves: and I take these differences and make them bigger. I use fear, distrust, and envy for control purposes. These methods have worked on my modest plantation in the West Indies and it will work throughout the South. Take this simple little list of

---

[1] http://matah.com/Lynch While the validity or veracity of this letter cannot be proven there is much evidence available from the life experiences of African -American men in American to substantiate the truth of those concepts mentioned in the letter. African-American men are suffering from the residual effects of slavery even into this century and our times.

differences, and think about them. On top of my list is "Ave," but is there only because it starts with and "A:" the second is "color" or shade, there is intelligence, size sex, size of plantations, status on plantation, attitude of owners, whether the slaves live in the valley, on a hill, East, West, North, South, have fine hair, coarse hair, or is tall or short. Now that you have a list of differences, I shall give you an outline of action-but before that I shall assure you that distrust is stronger than trust and envy is stronger than adulation, respect, or admiration.

This method of division is still present within the Black community and is reflective of Lynch's following prediction:

The Blacks, after receiving this indoctrination shall carry on and will become self re-fueling and self–generating for hundreds of years, maybe thousands. Don't forget you must pitch the old Black male vs. the young Black male, and the young Black male against the old Black male. You must use the dark skin slaves vs. the light skin slaves and light skin slaves vs. the dark skin slaves. You must use the female vs. the male, and the male vs. the female. You must also have your white servants and overseers distrust all Blacks, but are necessary that your slaves trust and depend on us. They must love, respect and trust only us. Gentlemen, these kits are your keys to control. Use them. Have your wives and children use them, never miss an opportunity. If used intensely for one year, the slaves themselves will remain perpetually distrustful. Thank you, gentlemen.[2]

The above strategies shared by Willie Lynch with the American slave owners had a very devastating effect on the African American

---

[2]   Ibid.

family. It destroyed the structure of the family, and emasculated the men by proving their incompetence in protecting and supporting their family and community. The current conditions of African American males reflect the residual effects of these practices and account for the inactive role that they play in the church and community. It also explains the distrust of the church and its leaders. The practices introduced by Lynch were deceitfully implemented in the name of God, and the church neglected to protect the men. Nor did the church attempt to salvage the purity of Christianity and distinguish the Word from the evils of men.

Presently harm continues to he inflicted upon African American men through institutional racism in America. Through violence, disproportionate imprisonment, and unemployment or underemployment, African American males are statistically disadvantaged in this country. Even those who are not susceptible to these specific conditions are still vulnerable in one form or another. The goal for developing a male mentoring manual is to protect African American males in a way that should have been done so long ago. By equipping those with godly guidelines and lifestyles to overcome systemic racism, the church may begin to win their trust and faith again.

The historical foundation of this project also parallels that of its social science foundation. In an anthology of the black family; Lee June and Matthew Parker draws on various writers regarding the residual effects of slavery, systemic racism, and oppression. The authors further support the significance of this project by revealing the way African Americans have been misunderstood in their plight to overcome the residual and ongoing effects of the American Slave experience:

> Casual observers often assume that Blacks have had social experiences that closely resemble those of their own ethnic group. To illustrate, other ethnic and racial groups will often say that their ancestors

overcame prejudice, discrimination, poverty, and oppression-so why cannot Blacks do the same? This type of thinking ignores pertinent sociological evidence (Feagin, 1984). The sociological experiences of Black Americans are not comparable to those of any other ethnic group in the United States, despite social science prognostications to the contrary (Lieberson, 1980).[3]

In the following excerpt, June and Parker continues to sustain the validity of this project specific focus on African American males:

> Blacks alone have experienced the irreparable complications of attempted genetic genocide, of being uprooted from their ancestral families and simultaneously deprived of names, culture, legacy, inheritance, and sponsorship from the old country. Blacks alone have survived the vicious dehumanization of slavery across generations, only to find themselves ushered into segregation and economic dependency by a society unwilling to make appropriate restitution for its atrocities against them. Blacks alone have watched as their labor, creativity, and productivity have been exploited from generation to generation. No other ethnic group has come close to this pariah status (Omi and Winant. 1986).[4]

In addition, African Americans have also experienced a division in their families by the social agencies in our urban cities. It was a matter of policy for these agencies to demand that the husband or father of children in a family relying on federal assistance be removed from the home. A violation of this policy could result in the families being expelled from the assistance program.

---

[3]   Lee N. June and Matthew Parker, eds., *The Black Family* (Grand Rapids: Zondervan Publishing House, 1991).
[4]   Ibid, 18.

The African American male faces many social problems regarding the African American family. In the novel, *Teaching Our Men Reaching Our Fathers,* Matthew Parker raises significant social science questions and offers some beneficial ministerial support and solutions to address some of these problems.

The African American Man and Lane's discussion on four basic needs: Admittedly, we must first make sure that they come and that they are sufficiently attracted to our churches, organizations, and programs to make the effort to participate.[5]

The best way to reach African American male adults is by one-on-one interaction. Men will not always respond to even the most fervent appeals from the pulpit. Hence men who are connected to Christ and to a local church family must make the effort to evangelize to other men at work and within the community. The best way for that to be done is through "relationship evangelism," As a man, one must make the effort to form friendships that surpass the level of superficiality and encourage a mutual relationship of spiritual sharing and growth.

This project is validated through its biblical foundation in that the scripture emphasizes the role of righteous men in many of its narratives. One narrative is that of the nation of Judah. Judah shared the plight of the absence of men in the book of Ezekiel. And I sought for a man among them that should make up hedge and stand in the gap before me for the land that I should not destroy it but I found no one.[6] Other narratives include that of Sodom and Gomorrah, where God reveals the significance of the presence of righteous men in the community: "So the Lord said, 'If I find in Sodom fifty righteous within the city, then I will

---

[5]   Matthew Parker, *Teaching Our Men Reaching Our Fathers* (Detroit: Matthew Parker, 2000), 40.

[6]   Ezekiel 22:30

spare the whole place on their account.'"[7] In the story of Rahab family's, [8] posterity and blessing of the land, was spared in return for her intervention on behalf of two righteous men: "And the city shall be under the ban, it and all that is in it belongs to the Lord: only Rahab, the harlot and all who are with her in the house shall live, because she hid the messengers whom we sent.'"[9]

The biblical foundation of this project also serves as a guide.[10] Paul writes to Timothy and provides a discipling model that guides the development of a manual, equipping men to mentor men: "And the things which you have heard from me in the presence of many witnesses, these entrust to faithful men, who will be able to teach others also."[11] The aforementioned narratives and the guide of 2 Timothy will be used as a blueprint for this manual's biblical foundation.

Theologically, this project is supported by the presupposition that it requires a man to mentor a man. As iron sharpens iron, so one man sharpens another."[12] There is both a passion and urgency at work in the development of this project. The power of the gospel for impacting individuals provides great promise to the local church, families, and communities. The project is a direct attempt of "the acceptable year" declared by the Lord in the following poignant text,

> The Spirit of the Lord is upon me, because he hath anointed me to preach the gospel to the poor; he hath sent me to heal the brokenhearted, to preach deliverance to the captives, and recovering of sight to

---

[7]   Genesis 18:26
[8]   Joshua 6:17-23
[9]   Ibid.
[10]   2 Timothy 2:20
[11]   2 Timothy 2:2
[12]   Proverbs 27:17

the blind, to set at liberty them that are bruised. To preach the acceptable year of the Lord.[13]

This project, therefore, seeks to develop a mentoring manual that results in men who are transformed,[14] conformed,[15] and represent the new creation.[16] These African American men will become leaders in the local church, strengthen their families, and act as catalysts of change in the community.

Significant Terms

1. <u>Mentoring</u> - John C. Crosby defines mentoring as "a brain to pick, a shoulder to cry on and a kick in the pants." Mentoring is the process of developing a person to his or her maximum potential in Christ Jesus. Paul Stanley and Robert Clinton define mentoring as "a relational experience (advice, wisdom, experience, habits, and principles) in which one person empowers…another by shaping them through God's given resources."[17]

   <u>Mentoring</u> - In their book, *Connecting: The Mentoring Relationship You Need to Succeed in Life*, Paul Stanley and J. Robert Clinton define mentoring as "a relational process between a mentor, who knows or has experienced something and transfers that something (resources of wisdom, information, experience, confidence, insights. relationships, status, etc.,) to a mentoree, at an appropriate

---

[13] Isaiah 61:1; Luke 4:18
[14] Romans 12:1,2
[15] Romans 8:29
[16] 2 Corinthians 5:17; Galatians 4:19
[17] Robert Vann, *Principles for Effective Mentoring of Ex-prisoners* (Washington: Prison Fellowship, 1998), 26-27

time and manner, so that it facilitates development or empowerment."[18]

2. Mentoree - A man who is in a healthy relationship with another man as a mentor.

Context

The context of this project is Bethany Baptist church of Detroit, Michigan and its community on the west side of Detroit. The church and its community are predominantly African American. The church has a roll of 300 members, but only about 150 or 50% of the members attend on a regular basis. The ratio of women to men in the Bethany Baptist church congregation is 4 to 1. Most of the congregation is comprised of elderly married couples and widowed females who have retired and are on fixed incomes. Some members are elderly widowers also living on fixed incomes. Others are young married couples with children, divorced mothers with children, single mothers with children, and very few single young men.

The majority of the men living in the church's Westside community are living in their parents' home or group homes. A small percentage of the males in this community live with their wives and children. The children of this neighborhood attend the local schools. These schools struggle to provide a quality education and are part of a public school system that has been taken over by the state governor with a board made up of members selected by the state and the mayor of the city. The school system is experiencing financial, academic and structural challenges. The major challenge is economic because of a decrease in the population of middle class citizens who provide a sufficient tax base.

---

[18] Paul Stanley and Robert Clinton, *Connecting: The Mentoring Relationships You Need to Succeed in Life* (Colorado Springs: NavPress, 1992), 40.

Many citizens have left the city to live in surrounding suburbs to seek better housing, living conditions, and a better education for their children. The flight of community members from the city to the suburbs has caused a strain on the urban environment of Detroit and its remaining families. Consequently, there are prevailing issues impacting the families in the Bethany Baptist Church and its Westside Community.

There are economic and educational differences between those men in the church and those of its Westside community who don't attend. The men in the church, on average, have a high school diploma: some of them have college degrees, and two are professionals. The men in the community reflect the demographic data for that area, which states that they have less than a high school education, and are often unemployed or underemployed according to the 2000 census. Most do not have a high school education, and many are living below poverty level. Some of them have had encounters with the legal system, and have criminal records. Others, have been engaged in substance abuse, and are not able to obtain gainful employment. The concentrated poverty, crime, unemployment, and lack of education have contributed to the emotional and health challenges of African American men living in this community.

This project seeks to empower men through a mentoring training program that is based upon the Word of God. The Word of God teaches us that godly men are blessed by the Lord with success and effectiveness:[19] This project seeks to contribute resources to the community by developing a program and a process by which the men of this community can be empowered. While the church cannot address all of the issues that have been raised, the church is empowered by God to make an impact through its witness and the proclamation of God's Word. The

---

[19]   Psalm 1

Word assures the people of God that all things are possible, and nothing is too hard for God:[20]

Procedure

The development of the mentoring manual was completed in three phases. After the observation was made that there was a serious shortage of men in the Bethany Baptist Church congregation, a random survey was made of African American pastors in the Mid-West Area of the United States (see appendix 1). The survey solicited general responses from urban pastors with African American males in their congregations. The questions regarded ministries specifically focused on African American men. Those pastors who had experienced success with their men were asked to share their ideas and methods. The data from the pastors' surveys, and literature reviewed served as the basis for the mentoring manual development.

The second phase of the procedure was to survey African American men in the Detroit Metropolitan Area. The primary focus of the survey was to generate a list of needs identified by the men taking the survey (see appendixes 2 and 3). The responses to these questions by the African American men and the information shared by those pastors surveyed, contributed to developing the mentoring manual.

The final phase of the project was to have pastors of successful African American male ministries to evaluate the mentoring manual. Non-pastors, writers, and researchers also evaluated the manual. The response to these evaluations indicated the strengths and weaknesses of the manual.

---

[20]   Philippians 4:13. NIV

Goals and Assessments:

Project Goal

The objective of this project is to create an effective manual that will increase male attendance and active participation of African American men in the church. The manual will be an effective tool to guide the mentoring of men by men. As a result of men being trained by their mentors who are equipped with spiritual values and guidelines, the mentorees will become active participants in the church. Upon completion of the mentoring training, both the mentors and mentorees will have better relationships with one another and with the church, having a desire to participate in church activities. After training the men, they will have a new understanding of what it means to be a godly man by studying godly characters in the Bible. They will learn what it means to be committed and devoted to the church by learning the Word of God and the demands God places on one's life. Men will also learn what it means to be bonded and related to other men as they make their journey through the mentoring process. Essentially, the behavior of the men will change positively toward the church, because their lives will be changed through the mentoring process.

Personal Goals

I will have an increased awareness of the plight of African American men in our society. I will have learned about the need for special focuses and emphasis on male ministries in the church. I will spend more time mentoring to my son and other men in my family. I will be more intentional in my efforts to mentor to other men in my profession as a judicatory leader.

Design and Procedure

The goals of the project are to increase attendance and active participation of men in the church. A survey of men in Bethany

Baptist Church and its community on Westside of Detroit will be conducted to determine their prior relationship with the church and church leaders. The same men will be surveyed after the mentoring training to determine the level of impact and change as a result of the mentoring process. The men chosen for the survey were those attending the Bethany Baptist Church and those men residing in the church's Westside Community

The pastors chosen for the survey were local pastors and those with ministries in the Mid-West Region of the United States. These pastors were chosen because the writer had access to necessary information about their ministries, their locations, and affiliations. Many of the pastors surveyed responded immediately and thoroughly along with offering helpful comments. These same pastors were given the completed mentoring manual for an evaluation. The writer's first contact with some of the African American men in the community was in the hospital while completing a hospital tour as a part of Clinical Pastoral Education training. The validity of the perceived need for a mentoring manual stemmed from these encounters. The injuries sustained by these men were often the result of violent interactions with other African American males. This is interpreted as a need for the establishment of healthy relationships between males within the African American community. The men needed to learn how to love, care and nurture each other. The need to develop the mentoring manual became more than a project, it became a passion.

Oral and written interviews provided insight into the African American males' opinion regarding relationships with God and church. Invariably, their opinions of God were favorable, but their opinions of the preachers and pastors were negative. Most of the men interviewed had low opinions of the pastors, and they did not trust them. The African American males who had positive opinions of the church and pastors were usually those active in church and had a position of leadership.

The pastors surveyed provided recounts of their experiences and insight into programs that minister to African American men. Pastors were able to agree or disagree with suggested programs for men identified in the survey. The survey responses from pastors revealed those programs that were successful, and those that were not. Pastors indicated the differences between churches with programs focusing on men ministries versus those that don't. Most of the pastors that were surveyed agreed that there should be an intentional and purposeful attempt to minister to African American men in the church and community. Some of those pastors with effective African American men ministries indicated that shared leadership with the men is essential

The pastors indicated that the attendance of men in the church increases when the pastors expressed a need for the men to be actively involved in the ministries of the church. They offered the opportunity for the men to participate at all levels of leadership and shared responsibilities. Those churches that did not make the adjustment and appeal to the men did not have an increase in attendance or participation. My goal was the development of a mentoring manual based on the information gathered from the surveys.

The development of this mentoring manual project proceeded in three phases. First, a survey of African American pastors (see appendix 1) was conducted. The pastors surveyed responded to questions regarding their male ministries. Those pastors with successful male ministries were offering programs similar to a mentoring model. Those pastors without men ministries experienced low attendance and participation. It appears from the African American men responses in the surveys that men are attending those churches where needs have been expressed and met, and they have shared experienced and shared leadership.

A survey of African American men was conducted in the Bethany Baptist church, the community surrounding the church, and a local hospital (see appendix 3). The men that were surveyed generally had poor opinions of the church, the pastor, and those men who attended the church. Some of the men felt that church was for women and children, and was not relevant to men. Others felt that the church did not reach out to men and neglected to meet their needs. Those African American men, who spoke positively concerning the church, were once active in church. The third phase of the assessment model involved those pastors in phase one of the project with successful male ministries. They were asked to evaluate this mentoring manual once completed.

Other pastors, researchers, authors, and those in male ministries will also be asked to evaluate this mentoring manual. A final survey will be done by those men completing the mentoring process (see appendix 7) to determine the impact of mentoring on their attendance and active participation in the church.

Plan of the paper

This first chapter has introduced the reader to the project. The following chapters will include a biblical, historical, and theological foundation in chapter two. Chapter three will focus on a review of contemporary literature. Chapter four will be a detailed description of the methods, procedure, and the design used in the project. Chapter five will be the results, and chapter six will be a reflection on the findings and implications of the project as it applies to ministry.

CHAPTER 2

Biblical, Theological, and Historical Foundations

Historically, the church has been a place of worship by men and women equally. Presently, it has become a place mainly attended by a majority of women and children. African American men are conspicuously low in attendance in the church. The need for more men to become active participants in the church is critical and essential to the health and success of its ministry. The African American church cannot carry out its mission effectively without the attendance and participation of African American men.

The biblical and theological basis for using mentoring as a method by which men can mentor men is supported with several scriptural passages. Mentoring was practiced in the Scriptures when Abraham mentored his nephew, Lot.[21] Mentoring was evident when Moses was exiled to Midian. His father-in-law, Jethro, mentored him.[22] Moses gave the foundation for training mentors in the book of Deuteronomy when he taught the Jews to obey God, and teach the commandments and statues to one another. Those statues and lessons are found in the Shema.[23]

> These are the commands, decrees and laws the Lord your God directed me to teach you to observe in the land that you are crossing the Jordan to possess, so that you, your children and their children after them may fear the Lord our God as long as you live by keeping all his decrees and commands that I give you, and so

---

[21] Genesis 11:12. NIV
[22] (Exodus 2 and 3)
[23] Deuteronomy 6:1-10. NIV

that you may enjoy long life. Hear, O Israel, and he careful to obey so that it may go well with you and that you may increase greatly in a land flowing with milk and honey just as the Lord, the God of your fathers, promised you. Hear, O Israel: The Lord our God, the Lord is one. Love the Lord your God with all your heart and with all our soul and with all your strength. These commandments that I give you today are to be upon your hearts. Impress them on your children. Talk about them when you sit at home and when you walk along the road, when you lie down and when you get up. Tie them as symbols on your hands and bind them on your foreheads. Write them on the doorframes of your houses and on your gates.

Jesus Christ in Luke, chapter 4, expressed the biblical mandate as Isaiah lifted his ministerial goal up first. Jesus makes the announcement that the focus of his ministry will be on the poor the oppressed the sick, and the captive. The verses found in the gospel of Luke, indicates that the followers of Christ, specifically the church, should actively participate in the delivery of good news to the poor, healing to the brokenhearted, deliverance to the captives, and recovery of sight to the blind.[24] The plight of some men in our culture and in our churches makes it a biblical and moral imperative for the church to actively engage in a search and rescue mission. Once found, the men need to be saved, healed, restored, and redeemed through the process of mentoring.

Several scripture verses teach us to seek men and to hold them accountable as spiritual leaders in their families. The men of God were to be sober-minded, upright, and blameless. The Christian men are to be role models in the community and in their homes.[25] God created man in his own image and likeness, and appointed him over the earth. Man is also called upon to leave his mother

---

[24] Luke 4:18–20. NIV
[25] Titus 1:6; 2:2. NIV

and father and be united as one with his wife.[26] God calls men to be prayerful, lifting up holy hands and to be without anger or disputing. Paul explains to Timothy the characteristics that are desirable in men called to the ministry, but these characteristics are also required of male leaders in the church. Every male leader should be responsible and faithful.[27] God calls men to love their wives as Jesus loved the church and gave himself for it. As fathers, men are called upon by the Lord not to exasperate his children, but to bring them up in the training and instruction of the Lord. [28] First, men are called to be accountable to God. Secondly, men are called to be accountable to each other. This mentoring manual for men is a method by which men can be mentored in the Bethany Baptist Church and its Westside community.

In the New Testament, there is a particular Scripture verse mentioned that provides a foundation for this mentoring manual. Mentoring is practiced by the way in which men relate to each other and carry each other's burdens. It is also hearing each other's struggles and pain. When men invest the time and connect emotionally to each other, they have fulfilled the Law of Christ.[29]

The scriptural foundation upon which mentoring African American men is based is established throughout the Old and New Testament. The care given by men to other men will be documented in the mentoring manual. The sharing of each other's stories and experiences will help to build relationships.

The population of men at the Bethany Baptist Church is disproportionately lower than that of women. A cursory survey was given to those pastors of a close fellowship and a random selection of other pastors. The responses confirmed the hypothesis that there is usually a larger female attendance in comparison to male attendance in many churches. However, it was revealed that

---

[26]   Genesis 2:18–25. NIV
[27]   1Timothy 2:8; 3:8-13 NIV
[28]   Ephesians 4:5. NIV
[29]   Galatians 6:2. NIV

congregations with maintaining healthy relationships. Even so, African American men cannot use the past to justify remaining in unhealthy relationships. Men can unlearn behavior that is injurious, and learn healthy behavior that is productive.

It is frighteningly difficult for an African American man to maintain his sanity in America. Many minority men are bombarded by sick and racist attacks in almost every phase of his emotional, physical and spiritual development. There is never a time when race is not an issue for a black man in many places in America. Many African American men can identify with the scenario of stepping onto all elevators occupied by a white female, who immediately withdraws to the wall of the elevator and clutches her purse. The African American man can be dressed in the finest business attire with a professional brief case in hand, and it won't make any difference, because the white woman is responding to the myths and stereotypes. When many African American men walk into the department store, he attracts a crowd. It could be the sales clerk, or it might be the security, but the African American man is perceived as a dishonest customer requiring constant surveillance. The African American men are stopped routinely in the urban community by the police (racial profiling), and specifically in the suburbs. He is always under the kind of scrutiny that no other ethnic group must suffer. He is often experiencing anger, rage and powerlessness from the humiliation he endures. Many African American men are depicted in the media as a menace to society. Consequently, mentoring given by the people of God can address those issues impacting African American men through an effective training process.

In the book of Jeremiah a similar anguish and frustration is expressed:

> The harvest is past, the summer has ended, and we are
> not saved. Since my people are crushed. I am crushed:
> I mourn, and horror grips me. Is there no balm in

Gilead? Is there no physician there? Why then is there no healing for the wound of my people?[30]

The "gospel of the Kingdom"[31] is the balm that heals. Listen to the hometown sermon of Jesus when he reads from the scripture:

> The Spirit of the Lord is on me, because he has anointed me to preach good news to the poor. He has sent me to proclaim freedom for the prisoners and recovery of sight for the blind, to release the oppressed to proclaim the year of the Lord's favor.[32]

The previous texts and the following scripture support the practical application of pastoral care. The prophets cautioned the people of God about neglecting to take care of one another and to make provisions so that the community of faith could be whole. Jesus lived out the mission of pastoral care when he went to the cities to free the captives, heal the sick and bind up the broken hearted. The text provides the theological foundation for this project. Mentoring is intended to offer healing and the process for men to develop healthy relationships.

Theological Basis

The theological basis for this project is men's relationship with God and his fellow man. Theology is defined as the knowledge of God and the supernatural.[33] It is religious knowledge and belief. Theology can be divided into two categories. It can be speculative or theoretical (the analysis of a set of facts in the ideal relation to one another) and practical or applied (using and adapting abstract principles and theory in connection with concrete problems). This

---

[30]   Jeremiah 8:20-22. NIV
[31]   Matthew 9:35. NIV
[32]   Luke 4:18-19. NIV
[33]   Webster's Collegiate Dictionary, 5th Edition

project will focus on using the practical or applied theology in connection with the concrete problems of African American men.

Rev. Seward Hiltner defines "Pastoral Theology," as that branch or field of theological knowledge and inquiry that brings the shepherding perspective to bear upon all the operations and functions of the Church and the minister and then draws conclusions of theological order from reflection on these observations".[34] Hiltner says that all of the functions of the minister are pastoral with the exception of preaching. The theology of pastoral care is lived out in the life of Jesus Christ in Matthew:

> And Jesus went about all the cities and towns, teaching in their synagogues, and preaching the gospel of the kingdom, and healing every disease, and every infirmity.
>
> And going, preach, saying; The kingdom of heaven is at hand. Heal the sick, raise the dead, cleanse the lepers, cast out devils; freely have you received, freely give.[35]

It is clear from God's word, and God's actions, that God cares about men having a relationship with God and one another. Mentoring has the goal of leading men to have relationships with God and each other. Mentoring has to address whatever needs are displayed by men so that they can be in healthy relationships. The power and effectiveness of mentoring has a biblical and theological history in the Scriptures: Abraham mentoring to his brother's son, Lot. He mentored Lot from childhood to adulthood, and he risked his own life and resources to rescue and restore Lot:[36]

Early in the Scriptures, we see God mentoring the Israelites. God spoke his Word through the prophets to teach his people.

---

[34] Rev. Seward Hiltner, Preface off Pastoral Theology (Nashville: Abington, 1958)20.
[35] Matthew 9:25; 10:7-8.
[36] Genesis 13,14 NIV

They were told to learn the Word of God, and to mentor to their children by teaching them continuously.

> These are the commands, decrees and laws the Lord your God directed me to teach you to observe in the land that you are crossing the Jordan to possess, so that you, your children and their children after them may fear the Lord your God as long as you live by keeping all his decrees and commands that I give you, and so that you may enjoy long life.
>
> Hear O Israel, and be careful to obey so that it may go well with you and that you may increase greatly in a land flowing with milk and honey, just as the Lord, the God of our fathers, promised you.
>
> Hear O Israel: The Lord our God, the Lord is one. Love the Lord your God with all your heart and with all your soul and with all your strength. These command that I give you today are to be upon your hearts. Impress them on your children. Talk about them when you sit at home and when you walk along the road. When you lie down and when you get up. Tie them as symbols on your hands and bind them on our foreheads. Write them on the doorframes of your houses and on your gates.[37]

The above scripture is indicative of God's intentional process for mentoring the Israelites with the Word and they were commanded to do likewise with their children as often as possible. God mentored to the adults, and the people mentored to the children. Mentoring takes place in the Bible as God instructs Moses to mentor Joshua.

> So the Lord said to Moses, take Joshua son of Nun, a man in whom is the spirit, and lay your hand on him. Have him stand before Eleazar the priest and

---

[37]   Deuteronomy 6:1–9 NIV

the entire assembly and commission him in their presence. Give him some of your authority so the whole Israelite stand before Eleazar the priest, who will obtain decisions for him b inquiring of the Urim before the Lord. At his command he and the entire community of the Israelites will go out, and at his command they will come in.

Moses did as the Lord commanded him. He took Joshua and had him stand before Eleazar the priest and the whole assembly. The he laid his hand on him and commissioned him, as the Lord instructed through Moses.[38]

The Scriptures indicate the necessity of leaders preparing their successors and the people for change. It prepared everyone through the effective use of a mentoring process so that there was no rivalry or jealousy between Moses and Joshua. The effective use of mentoring is also demonstrated in the relationship between Elijah and Elisha.

Elijah understood that he needed to prepare his protégé to assume leadership:

When they had crossed, Elijah said to Elisha, "Tell me, what can I do for you before I am taken from you?" "Let me inherit a double portion of your spirit," Elisha replied. "You have asked a difficult thing, Elijah said, "yet if you see me when I am taken from you, it will be yours otherwise not." As they were walking along and talking together, suddenly a chariot of fire and horses of fire appeared and separated the two of them, and Elijah went up to heaven in a whirlwind. Elisha saw this and cried out, "My father! My Father! The chariots and horsemen of Israel!" And Elisha saw him no more. Then he took hold of his garment and tore them apart.

---

[38] Numbers 27:18-21. NIV

He picked up the cloak that had fallen from Elijah and went back and stood on the bank of the Jordan. Then he took the cloak that had fallen from him and struck the water with it. "Where now is the Lord, the god of Elijah?" he said. When he struck the water, it divided to the right and to the left, and Elisha crossed over.

The company of the prophets from Jericho, who were watching, said, "The spirit" of Elijah is resting on Elisha." And they went to meet him and bowed to the ground before him.[39]

In the above biblical stories, the transition of leadership proceeds without problems, because the mentors obeyed God's Word, and the mentorees were obedient to the mentors. There are also mentoring examples in the New Testament. The mentoring process is demonstrated in the relationship between Barnabas and Paul.

When he came to Jerusalem, he tried to join the disciples, but they were all afraid of him, not believing that he really was a disciple. But Barnabas took him and brought him to the apostles. He told them how Saul on his journey had seen the Lord and that the Lord had spoken to him, and how in Damascus he had preached fearlessly in the name of Jesus.[40]

Barnabas risked being ostracized by the other Disciples of Christ for Paul. He believed Paul's conversion experience, and he believed in Paul's calling to the ministry. Afterwards, Paul and Barnabas were assigned as missionaries together to Cyprus. Paul eventually became a great apostle and writer of 14 books of the New Testament.

---

[39]   2 Kings 2:9-15. NIV
[40]   Acts 9:26-27. NIV

Historical Tradition

The history and tradition of the church has been structural in the life of men. The church was the place where lives were changed because men were valued. It provided essential lessons and guidance to the families in which boys became men. For the African American family, the church was the place where children received positive messages about their identity and history. The church was the place where damaging messages from the larger culture were counteracted and dispelled. The church was foundational in the life of men historically, because it integrated faith Christian values and education to form a lifestyle.

Traditionally many men had the benefit of living among an extended family and in neighborhoods that offered a network of support and opportunities. The church was at the hub of those opportunities operating as a conduit to economic success and upward mobility. There were a number of churches in the Detroit community through which men received leads to occupational opportunities in the local factories. In fact, a few of those churches had direct relationships with the employment office. The men would take a note from the church to the factory's employment office as a reference for employment. In return, the church grew and prospered with the men who had obtained gainful employment. These men would send for their families from the South, and many would become tithing members of the churches.

In the book edited by Lee N. June and Matthew Parker, they state the following history of the Black church:

> The Black church has always been actively involved in the educational and social development of Black people. Because Black Americans were not permitted access to formal education, the majority of Blacks were illiterate when slavery was abolished. The Black church immediately established schools to educate its people. The Black churches believed that the task

of racial uplift, both educationally and morally, lay basically in the hands of Blacks themselves.

Consequently, their schools became the prime examples of that viewpoint (Paris, 1985).[41]

Black churches have always engaged in the education of its members and community. The church in recent years has taken the lead in developing programs geared specifically to the needs of African American males.

Several churches have felt the need for programs that focus exclusively on the development of young Black males. They include the Black Youth Project of Shiloh Baptist Church in Washington D.C. Through athletics, counseling, and academic tutoring, this project ministers to youths in Washington's "depressed" areas. Project IMAGE, a consortium of ten Chicago churches, seeks to strengthen the image, role, and presence of Black males in families, churches, schools, and communities through ecumenical, community-based programs that address the need for positive male influences among Black boys. Summerendipity, launched in 1986 at the Pilgrims' Hope Baptist Church in Los Angeles, which counsels youth groups, teaches young people the evils of drugs abuse and gang violence and the virtues of thoughtful career decisions, and generally helps them maximize their personal effectiveness.[42]

The tradition in the Black community is replete with activities and contributions made by the Black church in the life of the Black community. There is an expectation on the part of the Black community for the Black church to continue its history of

---

[41] Lee N. June and Matthew Parker, eds., The Black Family (Grand Rapids: Zondervan, 1991), 117-118.

[42] Ibid., 120.

meeting the needs of its members. The needs of the Black family with regards to the plight of the Black male is more critical today than any time in the history of the Black community. It is essential for the church to respond to the crisis of the Black male. June and Parker made the following observations:

> As the oldest and most influential institution controlled by the Black community, the Black church has a crucial educational and spiritual role to play in the development of Black youth. The church will inspire and encourage youth as its programs and ministries are culturally relevant and applicable to real life needs and issues. As can be seen, many Black churches are rising to the challenge effectively, and with a serious sense of commitment. They are providing a wide variety of needed services and reaching large numbers of Black youth.[43]

The Black church is the only institution with a strong history of involvement in the life of the African American family. It is uniquely prepared to offer mentoring as a method of reaching the Black male. The biblical, theological and traditional history of the Black church makes it the most effective tool in the Black community for reaching men.

---

[43]   Ibid., 120.

CHAPTER 3

Review of the Literature

A review of the Literature concerning mentoring reveals that African American men must be reached through the church in an intentional and purposeful ministry that is holistic, continuous, and redemptive. William B. Oglesby Jr. offers a starting Point from which we can understand the importance of mentoring from a biblical perspective:

> In the biblical sense, mentoring is that function of the people of God wherein we "bear one another's burdens, and so fulfill the law of Christ" (Gal.6: 20) as the means for participating in the process of reconciliation. Pastoral counseling is rightly understood only in the context of mentoring and then at the more specific nature of pastoral counseling.[44]

Mentoring should be holistic in its approach with an objective of leading men to healthy relationships with God, other men, and women. Charles V. Gerkin establishes a biblical and theological basis for mentoring that begins with the religious roles of God's people in the Old Testament. Gerkin identities three models of mentoring:

> Our most reliable source regarding the beginnings of mentoring is, of course, the Bible. Turning first to that source, we learn that the care of the community of people, who worshiped the one God, Yahweh, required the assignment of leadership roles to certain

---

[44] William Oglesby Jr., Biblical Themes For Mentoring (Nashville: Abington, 1980), 39-40.

individuals. Our earliest pastoral ancestors are to be found among the leaders of the ancient people of Israel. From very early in recorded biblical history the custom was established of designating three classes of such leaders: the priests, a hereditary class that had particular responsibility for worship and ceremonial life; the prophets, who spoke for Yahweh in relation to moral issues, sometimes rebuking the community and its stated political leaders: and the wise men and women, who offered counsel of all sorts concerning issues of the good life and personal conduct.[45]

Mentoring has in the past and will in the future exist for the express purpose of providing care to the people of God. Gerkin, just as Wimberly, identifies the narrative approach to mentoring as a valid model for ministering to the people of God. In addition to a biblical and theological basis for mentoring this project also incorporates a cultural perspective.

The study of the African American male first requires a look at the African American family. Drs. George and Yvonne Abatso have done some comprehensive and extensive studies of the African American Family. They offer a summary of the plight of African American families in America from slavery to contemporary times Drs. George and Yvonne Abatso explain how the changes in the movements and migration of African American families from the South to the North, and from extended families to nuclear families have weakened the family and the church. They suggest that the church has to become equipped anew to deal with the contemporary problems that plaque the African American community. They identified the factors that have impacted the African American families:

---

[45]   Gerkins, Charles V., An Introduction To Mentoring (Nashville: Abington, 1997), 23

Today's Black family finds itself in a dilemma due to both external and internal factors, and the family is in a crisis. Statistics reflect trends in the condition of African American families. From 25 to 30% of all young Black males are either in prison or on probation, but supervised by the courts in some way. That is, at least 1/4 of Black youths are in jail or under the control of the judicial system. About 75% of African American children are being raised in poverty. Before Black babies are born, during the prenatal stage and throughout the first two years of life, the level and type of nutrition is directly related to their brain development. Many suffer from poor nutrition, and can he expected to develop related problems. Nutrition will affect their development in infancy and their ability to profit from schooling. Another factor affecting African American families is divorce. One out of three Black marriages ends in divorce. This adds to the number of families in which children will be reared by single parents. This also will affect their well-being, seeing that whether Black or white, single parents are at the bottom of the poverty scale.[46]

Again, the absence of men in general and African American men in particular, has a very negative impact on the African American family's survival. The focus on African American men through mentoring will strengthen the African American family and church. It is essential for the church to be intentional in reaching African American men if the church and community are going to become what it once was to the African American people. The African American community was positive in the midst of larger negative society. The African American community could offer

---

[46]   Abatso, George & Yvonne Drs. How to Equip the African American Family, (Chicago: Urban Ministries), 15-166.

support and encouragement to its members when it could not be found anywhere else. The church and community can reclaim its prominence and influence with the rescue of African American men. The holistic care for African American men through mentoring will address those issues of church membership and attendance relationship building. An approach to developing it holistic mentoring for men in the Bethany Baptist Church and its Westside community is "mentoring," A model of men mentoring men will be developed in a manual (see chapter 5).

A review of the literature indicates that there are existing models for increasing the attendance of men in the church, and there are models designed to disciple men in the community and in the church. Some of the models have been observed and evaluated by Dr. Larry L. Macon in his book, "Discipling the African American Male." Dr. Macon adequately evaluates those models and asserts that they attempt to deal with "family issues, male and female relationships, and the manhood of black men.[47] Those models were: Trinity United Church of Christ, Chicago Illinois; Oak Cliff Bible Fellowship, Oak Cliff, Texas; St. Paul community Baptist Church, Brooklyn, New York; and Concord Missionary Baptist Church, Dallas, Texas. All of these churches had successful men ministries says Dr. Macon, but they did not incorporate a training component that included men relating to women and children. Therefore, Dr. Macon's model was designed to include a component that taught men to relate to women and children. Dr. Macon mentions the need for the church to make Christ know to men through a mentoring process.

The objective will indirectly create healthier relationships between African American men and women. This project will focus on mentoring as a means of reaching men for Christ. There is a difference between discipling men and mentoring men. The

---

[47]   Larry L. Macon, Discipling The African American Male (Nashville: Winston Publishing, 1997)

difference is the degree to, which one commits to the relationship. Disciple and discipleship is defined as:

The term "disciple" is derived from the Koine Greek word mathetes, which means a pupil (of a teacher) or an apprentice (to a master craftsman), coming to English by way of the Latin discipulus meaning a learner while the more common English word is student. A disciple is different from an apostle, which instead means a messenger. While a disciple is one who learns from a teacher, an apostle is one sent to deliver those teachings or a message.

> Generally in Christian theology, discipleship is a term used to refer to a disciple's transformation from some other *World view* and practice of life into that of Jesus Christ, and so, by way of Trinitarian theology, of God himself. Note the Apostle Paul's description of this process, that the disciple "not be conformed to this world, but be transformed by the renewing of your minds, so that you can discern what is the will of God–what is good and acceptable and perfect."[48] Therefore, a disciple is not simply an accumulator of information or one who merely changes moral behavior in regard to the teachings of Jesus Christ, but seeks a fundamental shift toward the ethics of Jesus Christ in every way, including complete devotion to God. In several Christian traditions, the process of becoming a disciple is called *The Imitation of Christ*, and the ideal goes back to the Pauline Epistles. The influential book, *The Imitation of Christ* by Thomas à Kempis further promoted this concept in the 14th Century.[49]

This manual will use a more intimate and engaging relationship as a mentoring technique to reach men through men; Reviews

---

48   Romans 12:2
49   http://en.wikipedia.org/wiki/Disciple_(Christianity)#Discipleship

of the literature on mentoring covers many areas. Mentoring is used in the educational, corporate, and social settings. The research has shown that mentoring can be very successful with both men and women. Mentoring as a technique for reaching men in this project is used because of its history with being effective and appropriate for most people in need of guidance. Mentoring is also preferred because it can be applied to those men who have been damaged, discouraged, disappointed, dismissed, and requires a more intimate and committed approach. There are several mentoring models and programs in the areas of education, corporation, and religion.

Laurent A. Daloz, in his book *Mentor*, gives us an educational perspective on the actual term:

> We begin this chapter with a look at some ways, in which the term mentor has been used recently. Although mentors have always been around, in the years since Gail Sheehy popularized the term (in Passages, 1976) mentors have become increasingly visible. Success, we are told–whether in industry or academia–is a lot slippier without a mentor to show us the ropes. A flood of books and articles now proclaim mentors' virtues and defects (Speizer, 1981 Merriam, 1983; Gray, 1989; Bey and Holmes, 1992; Cohen, 1995; Luna and Cullen, 1997; Waters, 1998), And who has not read *Tuesday with Morrie* (Albom, 1997), that bittersweet journal of a young man and his dying mentor?
>
> Yet, relatively little work has been done on the deeper, metaphorical and archetypal context of the word. As we will see in a moment, it is of more than passing interest that the original Mentor was inhabited by Athena.

Daloz continues in detail about the characteristic of mentors and their relationships:

> Clearly, the mentor is concerned with transmission of wisdom. How, then, do mentors transmit wisdom? Most often, it seems, they take us on a journey. In this aspect of their work, *mentors are guides*. They lead us along the journey of our lives. We trust them because they have been there before. They embody our hopes, cast light on the way ahead, interpret arcane signs, warn us of lurking dangers, and point out unexpected delights along the way. There is certain luminosity about them, and they often pose as magicians in tales of transformation, for *magic* is a word given to what we cannot see–and we can rarely see across the gulf. As teachers of adults, we have much to learn from the mythology of the mentor.[50]

Daloz's writing and research focuses on the educational and business perspectives of the term "mentor," that are also applicable to this project. Daloz's research covers the origin of mentorship as it relates to older men mentoring younger men in mythology. He also writes that much of the mentorship has to do with the mentor traveling on the journey with the mentoree. He uses the story of *The Odyssey* as an illustration of mentorship:

In this book, Daloz has established the mentor as someone very special to the mentoree, and the relationship is continuous and transitional. The position of the mentor is also intergenerational as the mentor walks on the journey with the father and grandfather. The implications for the mentor in this project, is also one of transitions and intergeneration. The research establishes a foundation for the perpetual impartation that takes place in the mentoring process. It is the impartation or the pouring of oneself into another that makes the mentoring journey significant and life changing.

---

[50]   Laurent A. Daloz, *Mentor* (San Francisco: Jossey-Bass Publishers, 1999)

Daloz establishes the guidelines for creating a mentoring process that includes building a relationship with the mentoree, and walking on a journey with the mentoree in an environment of intimacy and trust. Daloz writes that mentoring is not limited to walking on the journey with the mentoree, but it also involves assigning tasks.[51] Mentoring is a process that requires time, commitment, and endurance on the part of both the mentor, and the mentoree. The process involves learning on the part of the mentor and mentoree, so that both benefit from the relationship, and both grow and continue to mature. Daloz writes in another book about the significance of the mentor in our lives. He says that if mentors did not exist, we would invent them.

Daloz considers the mentor as more than someone who walks with us on our journey, a mentor is someone who shares experiences and emotions with us, and because they have been where we aspire to travel.

Mentoring from an educational perspective is another approach to be reviewed. The author, Biddy Fisher, records the origin of mentoring, and its application in the library. He states how mentoring was applied historically by revealing the Greek version:

> Mentoring is not a new concept. The first mention of it and the titular hero of this book was an ancient Greek, chosen by Odysseus (Ulysses) to look after his son, the young Telemachus, while away on his epic voyage of discovery. There was more to the instruction than just keeping a paternal eye on the young man, and grooming Telemachus for his eventual position as head of state was a priority. This was achieved through advising, encouraging and teaching, by providing counseling and a role model, and passing on the experience, which the older man possessed to

---

[51]   Ibid. 217

the younger. It is also interesting to note that Greek mythology also allows for Mentors to be a woman and take the form appropriate to the situation via the goddess, Athena.[52]

In addition to the historical origin of mentoring, the author also gives a contemporary history of mentoring. Mentoring is used in today's society in the areas of education, business, and social institutions:

> American businesses were swift to understand the benefits for all if mentoring was promoted and encouraged. British business, cautious or even skeptical of the American management education, was slow to develop formal mentoring. However, it did rely for a large part on the 'old boy' network, not dissimilar to informal mentoring. It is now recognized that it needs more than serendipity or a gender-oriented network to ensure that employees are given the best opportunities for self and career development. Mentoring means formalizing a system that will assist the men who have experience in particular areas including the work environment. In this way it can have a significant effect on morale, motivation and quality of working life within an organization.[53]

The history of mentoring in the business environment has shared commonalities with mentoring in the educational and social institutions. There are some basic truths about the process regardless of the environment. The author of this book records the following observations:

---

[52]   Biddy Fisher, *Mentoring* (London: Library Association Publishing, 1994), 1.

[53]   Ibid. 2.

> Mentoring implies a certain relationship between individuals. Each mentoring arrangement will be unique, and its particular nature will be established according to the very personalities of the two individuals concerned. Mentoring is a learning process. It is part of the system in, which we engage, when life poses questions for which we are not prepared.[54]

The mentor must have characteristics such as intelligence, integrity, high personal standards, enthusiasm, and a willingness to share accumulated knowledge.

The role of the mentor is to counsel, advise, guide, model, and befriend the mentoree. This mentoring guide also indicates that the mentoring process should incorporate some essentials such as regularly scheduled meetings.[55] The meetings should take place in a comfortable environment where the mentor and mentoree feel at ease. This will encourage the development of a trusting, nurturing relationship. It is also essential for the mentor to possess social skills and enjoy developing a working relationship with others.[56]

Trisha Maynard and John Furlong's *Learning to Teach and Models of Mentoring* reveals several models for mentoring. The author introduces three distinct models, the first of which is called an apprenticeship model:

> This is an approach to learning to teach that is strongly advocated by O'Hear (1988) and the Hillgate Group (1989). In one of their more coherent passages, the Hillgate Group argue that there is a long tradition going back to Aristotle that some skills, including many that are difficult, complex and of high moral and cultural value, are best learned 'by the emulation of

---

[54] Ibid.2.
[55] Ibid., 4–5
[56] Ibid. 9.

experienced practitioners and by supervised practice under guidance' (p.9). In the case of such skills, apprenticeship, they suggest, should take precedence over instruction.[57]

The second model of mentoring in this literature is the Competency model–systematic training, and it is defined as follows:

> The mentor takes on the role of a systematic trainer, observing the trainee, perhaps with a pre-defined observation schedule and providing feedback. They are in effect coaching the trainee on a list of agreed behaviors that are, at least in part, specified by others.
>
> Systematic training in this country has a long history, becoming particularly popular in the 1970s with the development of interaction analysis, micro-teaching and somewhat tentatively in Circular 24/89 (DES, 1989) and now much more forcefully in Circular 9/92 (DPE, 1992).
>
> What is right about the competency approach is that after an initial period of collaborative teaching, trainees will benefit from an explicit program of training following a routine of observation and feedback. In this second stage of learning to teach, trainees must be given control of the teaching process. Learning at this stage necessitates trainees taking responsibility; they have to learn by actually doing the job of teaching. While still adopting some of the teachers' ready-made routines, they need to be helped progressively to form and implement some of their own while continually developing and modifying their own personal concepts and schemas. In order to help this process the mentor, therefore, needs at this

---

[57] Trisha Maynard and John Furlong, Learning to Teach and Models of Mentoring, ed. Donald McIntyre, Hazel Hag and Margaret Wilkin (London: Kogan Page Limited, 1993), 78.

stage of the trainee's development to take an active
role acting as a mirror or working as a coach.

Third and last model of mentoring in this literature from the
world of academia is the "reflective model-front teaching to
learning." This model is characterized as follows:

> In this final stage of practical preparation in teaching,
> trainees need to be encouraged to switch from a focus
> on their own teaching performance to a focus on the
> children's learning and how they can make it more
> effective. But to achieve this switch means more than
> the trainees simply extending his or her repertoire of
> routines. To focus on children's learning demands that
> trainees move beyond routines and rituals; they need
> to develop a deeper understanding of the learning
> process; thinking through different ways of teaching
> and developing their own justifications and practical
> principles from their work.
>
> While it is common for mentors to withdraw and
> let the trainees get on alone once they have achieved
> basic competence. It would seem to us that if mentors
> are to facilitate this shift of focus they must continue
> to take an active role. However, we would argue
> that trainees are unlikely to be ready for this form of
> reflection on their own practice until they have gained
> some mastery of their teaching skills; they need to be
> ready to shift their focus from their own teaching to
> the pupils' learning and that cannot come until they
> have gained some confidence in their teaching.
>
> Supporting trainees in this more reflective process
> necessarily demands a shift in the role of the mentor.
> To facilitate this process mentors need to be able to
> move from being a model and instructor to being a
> co-enquirer. Those other aspects of their role may
> continue but in promoting critical reflection a more
> equal and open relationship is essential. As we implied

earlier, thinking critically about teaching and learning demands open-mindedness and involves confronting beliefs and values. This is difficult and challenging work but we believe it is an essential element in what a true mentor must be.[58]

A continued review of this book on mentoring has revealed some characteristics of a mentor that can be a shared value to all who use a mentoring process. This following paragraph offers an interesting perspective on mentoring that could be true for many applications:

> In this world, where educationalists are being encouraged to use the language of business and the marketplace, the idea of being a 'mentor' risks becoming little more than a label to cover a new model of teacher training in which higher education is notable, like Odysseus for its absence- a kind of humane gloss, reassuring in its classical origins, for a profoundly inhumane conception of what is involved in learning to be a member of one of the most complex and demanding professions.
>
> By contrast, we want to take seriously the idea of a mentor as one who fulfills a highly humane, civilized and civilizing function. First of all, the mentor offers a model of what the trainee may someday become. We <u>do not say</u> 'a model of the professional teacher'; this kind of trite phrase, carving its own overtones of brisk, slightly detached superiority, is a good example of the influence of management-speak. Compare the reflex by, which in certain sorts of writing teachers are invariably called 'busy teachers'. There are other sorts of teacher to become; the 'busy teacher' is unlikely to make a good mentor. It takes *time* to listen.

---

[58]   Ibid., 82

There is also a table taken from this book review of "should" for the mentor that will he listed in (appendix 4).

A review of related literature on mentors in education depicted a view of mentoring from a negative perspective. This author tells the story of her educational journey that included encounters with racism at an early age by her elementary teachers. She relates how some of them impacted her with negative mentoring:

> I do not remember my first teacher's name, though I can still visualize her physical and emotional presence. She was a rather short European-American woman, probably in her forties, with short brown hair and glasses. She wore a white, short-sleeved blouse, and a beige skirt. She consistently told me to be quiet.

The quote above indicates that some tension may exist between the narrator and teacher. However, it is the quote below that explains the full extent of this tension:

> I continued to talk to her, to my peers, to myself. My excitement was overwhelming. I wanted to know everything that was to happen in this place called school. By mid-morning, I sat in a corner with my mouth plastered in off-white masking tape. I still see and feel the tears that streamed down my stinging cheeks. I did not remove the tape. I merely sat and watched as kindergarten progressed without me.

This feeling of frustration that the narrator describes while watching her classmates progress reveals the impact of the teacher, as a mentor, upon the student. Despite being of such a young age, the narrator describes feelings of isolation. The entire recall is full of overwhelming emotion.

I talked to myself about what school would be like the next day. When the bell rang, I was to walk home with a neighbor from my public housing complex. I decided not to join her. Instead, I remained on the playground and returned to my kindergarten classroom for the afternoon session. By the time my teacher realized I had not returned and prepared to call my home, my mother appeared at the door very concerned that something had happened to me. With much protest I was taken home. I remember the names of every one of my elementary school teachers except my kindergarten teacher. I only see her face.

The teacher's negative impact was powerful enough for the narrator to attempt memory block. However, it did not prevent the student from learning. The student remembered many things from kindergarten that were positive although her memories related to the teacher are negative:

At the age of 41, I have yet to feel any hate for her deed. I imagine I am numb to those feelings because I continue to remember scenarios from my kindergarten days. I remember the joy of learning, of drawing queens, of helping my cousin put on his snowsuit because he could not. I remember the teacher screaming throughout the year in efforts to terminate my perceived excessive chatter. I remember also my persistence in talking. I talked of learning and every wonderful experience of acquiring new knowledge. I never disrespected my teacher, in fact. I never said a mean word to or about her. She was a messenger of power. She represented learning, and I wanted every morsel available. My conduct grades were deplorable, while my academic grades were superior.

For many children, such an experience could have been traumatic in many nonproductive ways.

However, that kindergarten teacher was a negative mentor who attempted to and succeeded in silencing the persistence and resilience of my voice, instead of molding it.[59]

The perseverance of her learning ability despite negative conditions parallels the experience of successful African Americans. However, as in the case with African American males, the student would be even more prepared and better acclimated to society had the mentor met her needs.

Further review of the literature researched reveals the variety of methods by which mentoring takes place. Educational institutions use mentoring in various ways and to varying degrees. The following paragraph indicates how mentoring is used in one educational institution:

'Mentoring is traceable to *Mentor*, a trusted friend of Odysseus in Homer's *Odysseus*, who acted as a guide and counselor to Odysseus' son of Telemachus. Thus 'mentoring' generally refers to a supportive relationship between a novice and a more experienced guide. But meanings vary, partly due to the range of mentoring contexts within and across professions. For example, in noting the confusion over the term within nurse mentoring within the Health Service, Armitage and Burnard (1991) have suggested separation into two roles of mentor and preceptor. Within teacher education, McIntyre Hag–On and Willcin (1993) have acknowledged the lack of clarity about 'what the role is and should be', and what 'mentoring means' (p. 11). Mentor-like behavior may come from many

---

[59]   Carol A. Mullen, Maggie D. Cox, Cindy K. Boettcher, and Diane S. Adoue, Editors, *Breaking the Circle of One Redefining Mentorship in the Lives and Writings of Educators, Gwendolyn Webb-Johnson, My Emerging Destiny: Mentoring from an African American Perspective* (Peter Lang: New York, 1997), 5.

sources within a school, and the appointed mentor may engage in such unmentor-like activities as making formal summative assessments of students with career-shaping implications of 'passing' and 'failing'.[60]

A review of this book gives a comparison between coaching, counseling, and mentoring. The importance of this comparison can help the reader to make a distinction between the three, and to express their similarities. The explanation of the three models follows:

> Coaching best describes those processes that take place over a relatively short to intermediate time span. For example, a new employee is hired and is gradually trained to perform a particular job. Or a new team is formed, and members teach each other the various aspects of their jobs so that all understand the roles of the different team members and how these roles work together. Or a manager may need to acquire a new set of technical skills, and an associate may coach her during the learning process.
>
> Counseling invokes relatively short-term interventions designed to remedy problems that interfere with the employee's job performance. These short-term problems are usually considered to be motivational or attitudinal. We are not referring to what happens when employees are told by supervisors to improve or get out, but rather when an individual is having trouble succeeding and a respected peer helps the person see ways to overcome problems by trying some new behavior.
>
> Mentoring describes processes carried out over a long time span. A mentor is most helpful in facilitating overall career growth and personal advancement. The

60 Robin Yeomans and John Sampson eds., *Mentoring I the Primary School* (The Farmer Press: Washington, DC., 1994), 2.

mentor influences the associate by virtue of her ability to open doors to opportunity. We believe that good mentors deal with the complete life space and life structure of the mentee-family, career, and current work role.[61]

A review of this book on mentoring gives additional distinctions and comparisons between mentoring and other models of guidance. This author explains the difference between being a sponsor, role model, or mentor. The differences are explained as follows:

> A sponsor can be an active booster or advocate for any number of people, all at the same time. For example, a sponsor can finance the company baseball team recommend several candidates for promotional opportunities, or establish scholarship funds at the local university. A sponsor is constrained only by time and generosity. On the receiving end, a fortunate individual may have several sponsors. The sponsoring relationship is informal, with neither person making any commitments of responsibility or interaction. The sponsor most certainly knows who is being sponsored; however, the sponsored person may or may not know who the sponsor is. The sponsor role can continue indefinitely, as long as the sponsor sees a need and is willing and able to continue in the role.
>
> Role models can perform the same activities as a sponsor or can simply he held in high regard by any number of people without even knowing that they are viewed in this favorable light. Undoubtedly someone like Malcolm Forbes was a role model to hundreds of aspiring business students, whether they'd met him

---

[61] Oscar G. Mink, Keith Q. Qwen, and Barbara P. Mink, *Developing High-Performance People The Art of Coaching* (Addison-Wesley: Reading, 1993), 22-23.

or not. Similarly, an individual may have several role models at one time. There is no particular structure to the role-modeling relationship. It can continue as long as the observer sees positive behaviors to emulate.

Mentor. By contrast, in a facilitated mentoring process there is typically one mentor to one protégé, and each knows what is expected of the other. The mentor carries out some or even all of the functions of the sponsor and role model in a relationship structured around the skills that the protégé wants to develop.

Protégé. Popular labels for the protégé include mentee, candidate, apprentice, aspirant, advisee, counselee, trainee, and student. Less popular synonyms are follower, subordinate, applicant, hopeful, and seeker.[62]

Jawanza Kunjufu wrote a book about African American men. "Adam! Where are You?" this question refers to the lack of men in and around the church. The goal is to train the men within the church to extend relationships with the men outside of the church. According to the research done by Jawanza Kunjufu, there are some expressed reasons why men do not attend church.

The book *God's Armor Bearer* shares some insight into the selection process of a mentor. The writer of this book develops a definition of commitment for anyone answering the call of God in their life. The use of the commitment model in this text applies to the selection process for mentors as well. He explains the definition as follows:

> The first key to commitment is a loyalty and faithfulness that goes beyond all personal feelings. The dictionary defines loyalty as being "faithful to a prince of a superior, true to an alighted (vowed or sworn to)

---

[62] Margo Murray and Marna A. Owen, Beyond The Myths and magic of Mentoring (Jossey-Bass: San Francisco, 1991), 22-23

faith, duty, or love." Faithfulness is defined as "firmly adhering to duty, loyal, true to one's allegiance," or as being "a faithful subject."

These definitions show the heart of an armor bearer. This is someone willing to give of himself for others. He is dependable and loyal to his leaders and can be trusted with difficult assignments. Loyalty and faithfulness, of course, are first to God and then to man.[63]

Bill Hull's book, *The Disciple Making Pastor*, has very strong implications and contributions to development of the mentoring manual, because of its emphasis on integrity, accountability, and commitment. Hull's, gives as several examples of the committed pastor as follows:

> He/she is committed to placing disciple making at the heart of the church. He commits himself to the clear identification and communication of the roles of the pastor, the people, and the discipline process. He is committed to the priesthood of all believers. He has a commitment to multiplication.
>
> Without this kind of commitment, he/she will not move the people toward disciple making, much less lead them to become reproducing believers. It all starts at the heart of the matter - where lie places disciple making in relation to the church.

Hull places an additional emphasis of discipling on reproduction. The committed disciple has a heart for reproducing him or herself:

> "Having a heart for" is the same as "possessing a conviction concerning" the potential leader devotes himself or herself to disciple making because it is a product of the discipling process. Convictions are

---

63   Terry Nance, *God's Armor Bearer* (Tulsa: Harrison House, 1972), 37.

bone-deep beliefs hammered out in life experience. I know it intellectually, I've experienced it practically; therefore, it is a fundamental belief that governs my life.

A heart for disciple making burns with the desire to get into the harvest field and reap the harvest Jesus promised (Matthew 9:38). It means that the number-one priority is to make disciples, to find and spend time with eager learners who want to reproduce. This pastor sees disciple making as the fountainhead for effective, reproducing ministry. He/she believes that disciple making is the key to multiplication, and the Great commission will not be completed without multiplication.[64]

The desire for reproducing disciples expressed by this author is applicable to the mentoring process as mentors develop a burning desire to perpetuate their leadership. Mentoring is the establishment of a deeper and longer relationship than discipling.

Therefore, mentoring could be more effective than the traditional disciple model.

The next book reviewed is by Gary J. Oliver, *Real Men Have Feelings Too*. In this book, Oliver gives a compelling argument about the socialization process men have undergone in America that precludes them from acknowledging their feelings because it is a sign of weakness. Oliver asserts that men must he taught how to reconnect to their feelings and he made whole. The significance of man's emotions is stated below:

By now it should be clear that one of the most fundamental aspects of being a mature man involves our emotions.

However, many men are surprised to discover that the Bible has much to say about emotions. We

---

[64] Bill Hull, *The Disciple Making Pastor* (Old Tappan: Revell, 1988), 117.

have emotions because God has emotions. Emotions are intended by God and designed by God. From Genesis to Revelation we read about God's emotion: He is jealous, angry, loving, kind, and grieves over man's rebellion. And we are created in His image. That means, like God, we experienced and expressed anger, distress, sorrow, disappointment, frustration, fear, compassion, joy and delight.[65]

When men deny their emotions, they are denying an essential part that God has made. This author highlights the significance of men's emotions. An effective mentoring manual would have to deal with helping men get in touch with their emotions.

Another encouraging book reviewed is *From Age-ing to Sage-ing*. Zalman Schachter-Shalomi explains how America has neglected to take advantage of the wisdom of its elderly citizens by placing the most value on youth. He makes the following observations about the elderly in our society:

> Then what are elders? They are wisdomkeepers who have an ongoing responsibility for maintaining society's well-being and safeguarding the health of our ailing planet Earth. They are pioneers in consciousness who practice contemplative arts from our spiritual traditions to open up greater intelligence for their late-life vocations. Using tools for inner growth, such as meditation, journal writing, and life review, elders come to terms with their mortality, harvest the wisdom of their years, and transmit a legacy to future generations. Serving as mentors, they pass on the distilled essence of their life experience to others. The joy of passing on wisdom to younger people not only seeds the future, but crowns an elder's life with worth and nobility.[66]

---

65 Gary Oliver, *Real Men Have Feelings Too* (Chicago: Moody, 1993), 60.
66 Zalman Schachter-Shalomi, *From Age-ing to Sage-ing* (New York:

Schachter-Shalomi continues to make the case for mentoring by indicating the effectiveness of mentoring in the life of the younger generation. The mentor helps the mentoree to find his or her place in society on their own terms and individuality:

> Both The Karate Kid and Siddhartha illustrate the age-old practice of mentoring, the art of intergenerational bestowal by which elders pass on to younger people the living fame of their wisdom. As philosopher Martin Briber points out, in the crucible of this generative relationship, the elder helps forge a center in the younger person. Mentors do not impose doctrines and values on their mentees in an attempt to clone themselves. Rather, they evoke the individuality of their apprentices, applauding their as they struggle to clarify their values and discover their authentic life paths.

This book focuses more on the essence of mentoring than any other books reviewed. The author considers the entire process of mentoring and its impact on both the mentoree and the mentor. Schachter-Shalomi clearly identifies the sacrifice and investment made on behalf of the mentor in the life of the mentoree. The mentor knows how influential his or her life is and behaves accordingly:[67]

> To individuate to become our unique selves rather than secondhand imitations, we need someone standing behind us, saying as it were, "I bless you in the heroic, worthwhile, and difficult task of becoming yourself." Such a person evokes our questing spirit, not by giving answers, but by deepening our ability to question and to search for meaning. As we work through anxiety,

---

Warner Brooks, 1997), 12.

[67] Ibid., 189

life path, our mentor acts as a midwife, helping us breathe more easily as we give birth to ourselves in the world.[68]

John C. Maxwell, in *Developing The Leader Within You*, gives a perspective on mentoring training in the position of leadership. Maxwell explains how the mentor has influence and impact on those following him or her:

> A leader is great, not because of his or her power, but because of his or her ability to empower others. Success without a successor is failure. A worker's main responsibility is doing the work himself. A leader's main responsibility is developing others to do the work (see chapter 7). Loyalty to the leader reaches its highest peak when the follower has personally grown through the mentorship of the leader. Note the progression: At level 2 the follower loves the leader; at level 3 the follower admires the leader; at level 4 the follower is loyal to the leader. Why? You win in people's hearts by helping them grow personally.[69]

The need for this manual is the result of obtaining information, conducting an investigation, and making an observation that men are disproportionately represented in most congregations on Sunday mornings. The attendance of men was specifically less than that of women in the congregation of the Bethany Baptist Church in Detroit, Michigan. The idea for this manual was first conceived as a way for pastors and church leaders to seek, attract, and retain men in their congregations. The mentoring manual could address those issues that impact men in our churches and communities in an intentional and purposeful way. Some pastors

---

[68]   Ibid. 189

[69]   John C Maxwell, *Developing The Leader Within* (Nashville: Thomas Nelson, 1982), 9.

and congregations seemed to have accepted the status quo and had not developed an effective male ministry.

Men are essential to the healthy development and maintenance of the African American family, The following introductory statement from a book entitled "How to equip the Africa American Family," captures the essence of the African American male experience in today's society.

Today's Black Family finds itself in a dilemma due to both external and internal factors, and the family is in a crisis. Statistics reflect trends in the condition of African American families. From 25 to 30% of all young Black males are either in prison or on probation, but supervised by the courts in some way. That is, at least 1/4 of Black youth are in jail or under the control of the judicial system.[70]

Stephen B. Boyd writes that many men do not attend church nor have confidence in the church because the church has failed them as men. He writes that the church has avoided addressing the issues that impact men in very special and critical ways:

> Much of the stirring that is happening among men, however, is happening outside the institutional church. Why is that? I think there are several reasons. First, many men have been hurt by particular uses of Christian scriptures, symbols, and doctrines, which have sometimes been used to instill or, at least, reinforce masculine patterns of feeling, thinking, and acting that have been harmful to us and to others. Second, many hold us collectively and personally responsible for much past and present discrimination. Tom Wingo mentions three of our sins-and sins they are - racism, xenophobic militarism, and sexism. I would add homophobia/heterosexism, classism, and anti-Semitism. The problem is that we haven't

---

[70] George Abasto and Yvonne Abasto, *How to Equip the African American Family* (Chicago: Urban Ministries, 1991), 15.

gotten much help from the church or anywhere else in understanding how, for example, we came by our sexism, the specific ways it is destructive to women, how it is destructive also to men, and what, concretely, we can do about it. I would say the same thing about our homophobia/heterosexism, racism, classism, and anti-Semitism. Third, many of us have been trained to discipline our psyches and bodies to take whatever comes at us, repress or control our emotional responses, and go on with whatever task is before us. However, we haven't had much help from the church in understanding what has happened to us; how we have been hurt and mistreated and how we can heal so that we do not recycle that violence and mistreatment to others and to aspects of ourselves. In other words, the church has not always been a safe enough place for men to step out of their culturally defined masculine roles in order to redefine ourselves and those roles. For this reason, many men are turning to other cultural and religious traditions (African and Native American among others) for stories, rituals, and perspectives from which to experience needed transformation. Some are doing this with great effect, and I have learned and continue to learn much from them and from those traditions.[71]

The author appropriately states that he does not speak for all men because of his own limitations with respect to his ethnicity and experiences. He qualifies himself as a white man who is speaking from his culture, tradition, and experiences. However, he raises some very good issues that are applicable to all men in our culture. Men will not become effective mentors of other men until they have addressed those issues of fear as related to homosexuality, emotions, and masculinity.

---

[71]   Stephen Boyd, *The Men We Long to Be* (San Francisco: Harper, 1999), 12.

The book *Mother's & Sons* reveals how effectively boys and men can he mentored by mothers. Jean Lush has written about some famous men in history who were mentored by their mothers in the absence of a father either emotionally or physically. She writes about the following men:

> During his career, Jennie sent Winston books that molded his style of writing and speech. She used her enormous influence to get him transferred from one war to another, secured his early assignments as a war correspondent, and acted as his agent for his first stories and books. She campaigned alongside Winston in his early elections and opened doors to all the important people of his time. Most importantly, she gave him her courage and stamina.
>
> It took tremendous energy to raise Winston Churchill. Relatives saw him as a pesky nuisance. His teachers wailed that he was a failure.
>
> But, Jennie perceived his uniqueness and special needs, and rather than making him fit into a prescribed mold, she nurtured his personal interests.[72]

Jennie Churchill knew what was required of her to raise her son to become a man. She knew that he required love and patience, and she gave it. She knew that her son required structure and consistency, and she ease it. Mentoring requires all of those skills Churchill's mother used, and the Jean Lush writes about other mothers equally successful.

Susannah Wesley is another mother that made lasting impacts on the world, Susannah describes how she was able to mentor to her sons and contribute to their development into successful men. Susannah raised John and Charles Wesley by the following principles:

---

[72] Jean Lush with Pamela Vredevelt, Mothers & Sons (Tarrytown: Fleming H. Revell, 1988), 23-24.

Susannah maintained a strict schedule in her home and school, and was orderly and methodical in handling daily activities.

Her children were taught the importance of confession. When they did something wrong and fully confessed she did not inflict punishment, but praised them for their honesty.

She always rewarded obedience.

When it was necessary to discipline her children, Susannah was mild and kind, but very consistent. She never allowed their crying to manipulate her.

Loudness was not permitted in the house.

Respect for one another was a must. None of the children was permitted to invade the property of a brother or sister in the slightest. A pence or farthing (one cent) couldn't be touched if it belonged to someone else.

All promise made had to be kept.[73]

The above rules of Susannah Wesley are typical of many rules she enforced to raise 19 children. She was a very effective mentor who was able to deal with tragedy and adversity. Nine of her children died in infancy, and the family was often without adequate food and provisions. The authors' use of this woman as a mentor raises the bar for mentors considerably.

One of the greatest men to live in the 20th century was Martin Luther King Jr. He had a mentor who was also well known and respected throughout the world. That mentor is Benjamin H. Mays. He writes his autobiography and tells of some difficulties that challenged him in his life's journey. The following account of a racial incident by the author is indicative of the kind of mentoring he would have offered to Martin Luther King Jr.:

---

[73] Ibid., 26.

My second unforgettable racial experience during my high school years took place in Orangeburg, South Carolina. I was always eager to earn a little money by working for someone in town, or by assisting Mr. Davis, my painting instructor, on one of his jobs in the city. A friend of mine, Isaiah Kearse, was leaving a job and I wanted it, so I went to apply for it. I knocked on the front door and the man of the house came to the door and angrily asked me what I wanted. I told him that I had come to ask for the job that Mr. Kearse had. I had made two grave mistakes: I had come to his front door, and I had called my friend Mister. The man of the house called me a "black s.o.b." and warned me about ever coming to his front door. He made it clear that no Mister Kearse had worked there, but "Isaiah worked here; and if you want to see me go to the back door." I didn't go to the back door.

I left.

It was not enough for this man to refuse to call any Negro Mister: he wanted to dictate to me what I should call members of my own race. It is degrading enough to deny a man a title of civility because he is black; but to deny him the right to give titles to members of his own race is just going too damn far! I left that man's house in a hurry, no more fearful of what he might do to me than of what I might do to him. Once I realized that Negroes were frequently expected to go to the white man's back door. I never went to see anyone if the back door was a requirement. One has to rebel against indignities in some fashion in order to maintain the integrity of his soul.[74]

It appears that some of King's positions on disobeying unjust laws were a result of his mentor's influence. Benjamin E. Mays'

---

[74] Benjamin E. Mays, *Born to Rebel* (Athens: The University of Georgia Press, 1971), 46–47.

writings are very passionate and convincing as he relates his experiences in the segregated South and racist North.

The book by Laura Schlessinger, *Ten Stupid Things Men Do To Mess up Their Lives*, is based upon her own declaration that her book intends to reach three types of men: those that learn from reading, those that learn from the trials and tribulations of other men, and those that learn from personal electrocution.[75] Laura maintains that the stupidity of men is based upon their low opinion of women. Laura says men see women as helpless and needy and themselves as the rescuers and fixers. The distorted view men have of women causes them to behave "stupidly". While Laura's, book does not exhaust all stupid things men might do, it covers some important points deserving serious attention. Although this book lacks the positive reinforcement needed for the mentoring manual, it provides insight into issues that need to be addressed but are often overlooked.

Tex Sample writes a book about story telling. In *Ministry in an Oral Culture* he talks about the impact that oral tradition has in specific communities. It appears that all people have a history that is oral. Sample makes the following observation about the oral traditions of certain ethnicities:

> Let me be clear, too, that I am not talking only about Anglo-European whites. The powerful place of a traditional orality among African Americans, Hispanics, Native Americans, and Asians in United States society must not be forgotten. Indeed, part of the genius of the black church has been the continuity of its oral practices in preaching, worship, and other dimensions of congregational life. Henry H. Mitchell and Nicholas Cooper-Lewter speak directly to this

---

[75] Laur Schlessinger, *Ten Stupid Things Men Do To Mess Up Their Lives* (New York: Harper Collins, 1997), IX.

issue in their discussion of "soul theology" and the place of oral tradition in its practice.

Ronald B. Mincy was motivated to write his book, *Nurturing Young Black Males,* from personal experiences and personal losses. He considers himself to be fortunate having survived a neighborhood flooded with drugs, crime, and poverty. Mincy writes that he no longer is interested in identifying problems, but solutions:

> Finally, I changed. I stopped relying on the income policy and human services community to learn what I needed to know about the structure of interventions for young black males. I learned that there are policymakers, researchers, social service practitioners, and program officers in community and human development who are vitally interested in what is happening to young black males in high risk environments. In this volume I have asked members of this community to think collaboratively with me, to try to incorporate our collective knowledge about the human development needs and services relating to young black males into an income policy and human services framework.[76]
>
> It is a common observation that there are more African American men in prison than there are in Colleges or institutions of higher learning. It is astounding that the government will make more funds available to incarcerate African American men and maintain them as oppose to funding institutions of higher learning that could impact the rate of recidivism. It does not take a genius to make the discovery that if one is illiterate and unskilled when incarcerated, and released to the same environment

---

[76]   Ronald B. Mincy, *Nurturing Young Black Males* (Washington D.C.: The Urban Institute, 1994), 4

after serving a sentence, then one will probably return to the behavior that allowed them to have money and materials. It is never right or appropriate to indulge in criminal behavior, but there does not seem to be man's options for those who are poor, uneducated, untrained, and unsupported. This book offers some good insights and statistics on the plight of African American men, but it fails to offer a specific method by which one can engage the men and resolve the problems impacting them. A support system in the church with mentors could be an approach to end this vicious cycle.

Mincy has emphasized major factors that contribute to the poor state of African American males in this Society. He has addressed public policies that are cause for concern and implied a need for prioritizing of the political agenda in the excerpt above. He continues by offering ways to effectively meet the needs of African American males in the following quote:

> Clearly, the black men in America are in a crisis- and need to he embraced by the church in many nurturing and protective ways. There are some groups and organizations attempting to address the problems confronting African American men in Michigan. They are offering intervention in health and educational programs. But, the desperate and urgent situation requires something more than intervention. The church, guided by the Holy Spirit, can offer divine intervention. Authors George and Yvonne Abatso indicated that the African culture from which African American men came many years ago, did not make a distinction between the secular and the sacred. They said that life was approached holistically, and God was at the center of their lives. They suggest that African American men need to return to that tradition

and practice so that they can survive and revive the African American family.[77]

A review of the literature indicates that there have been mentoring programs in churches and church-based programs that have been successful. One of those programs, is the TOP (Transition of Prisoners) mentoring program located in Detroit, Michigan. The concept of TOP has been embraced by the Detroit community because it is effective. The program has a success rate with less than 18% recidivism.

The book used to guide the mentoring process in the TOP program is *Principles for Effective Mentoring of Ex-prisoners';* the author, Rev. Robert Vann, describes the purpose of the book as follows:

This book was designed as it ministerial tool to train mentors to assist ex-prisoners in an aftercare setting. Principles for Effective Mentoring is based on the first and second greatest commandments (Matthew 22:37-40) that are the scriptural foundation tor the concept of a relational learning process (mentoring).[78]

This book deals comprehensively with mentoring. It gives a historical, biblical, and contemporary use of the mentoring process. The book stresses the importance of relationships in the mentoring process throughout. It also makes a distinction between discipleship and mentoring. The following table is an example by Bob Biel:

---

[77] Ibid., 18-19.
[78] Robert Vann, *Principals for Effective Mentoring of Ex-Prisoners* (Washington, D.C.: Prison Fellowship, 2000), 2.

Discipleship	Mentoring
Biblical Model: Timothy	Biblical Model: Barnabas
Discipler is a teacher/professor	Mentor is an experienced friend/loving aunt or uncle image
Focus: Leader's agenda	Focus: Mentee's agenda
Focus: Spiritual disciplines	Focus: Whole life counsel
Interchange is based on content	Interchange is based on relationship
Usually short-term commitment	Ideally a lifetime commitment
Offers academic mastery	Offers practical life experiences
Requires only a respectful chemistry[79]	Requires positive personal relationship

---

[79]   Ibid., 22. The writer agrees with those who would argue that there is not distinction between the model of mentoring and discipling as practiced according to the scriptures. However, the writer is suggesting that the contemporary practice of discipling focuses on academics while mentoring goes deeper and focuses on relationship building with God and man.

CHAPTER 4
Methods, Procedures, and Research Design

Purpose

The purpose of this project was to develop a manual by which men could be trained to mentor other men. The goals of the project were to increase attendance of men in the church and to increase their active participation in the church ministries.

To accomplish the goal, the writer has developed mentoring lessons and began to train the men in the Bethany congregation. The men were trained to be mentors to other men. They were asked to commit to 10 weeks of training on Saturday mornings from 8:00 a.m. to 10:00 a.m. They were encouraged to be on time and to be in class each time the class met. The commitment was stressed so that the men could understand how crucial it was for them to become mentors to other men.

Overview

The initial step in the project was the observation that male membership and attendance in the Bethany Baptist Church was significantly less than that of women. The first thing that was done was to develop a survey of the men in the church and community. The survey was done to ascertain the reasons men do not attend church. The first survey was done orally and informally.

The interviewer was doing a unit of Clinical Pastoral Education, and was at the emergency room for several weekends. Most of the men surveyed orally, were in the emergency room of a local hospital. Usually it was other African American men that had injured the men in the emergency. When interviewed orally, most of the men exhibited negative impressions of the church and church leaders. They expressed a dislike and distrust of preachers and pastors. The men believed that the women were giving their money to the preachers, and that the preachers were wasting the money, or using it to fulfill personal desires.

After having done the oral interview, a written interview was developed and administered in the hospital, church, and the local East side community of the Bethany Baptist Church. The survey format used is located in the appendix.

Interviews of the pastors with successful male ministries revealed that men wanted shared leadership with the pastors, and a significant role in the church. The pastors with successful male ministries also had a specific focus on men in the congregation, and made special efforts to attract the men to the congregation, and they did specific things to maintain the men's attendance and participation. The responses from the interview with pastors and African American men aided the development of the mentoring manual.

Goals

The goals of the manual, was to train men to mentor other men so that there would be an increase in attendance at Bethany Baptist Church and also an increase in men participation in the activities in the church. The manual was designed to help men develop a relationship with God and with each other. The establishment of a trusting relationship is primary and essential in a mentoring process. The men were encouraged to share each other's life journey as a way of initiating conversation and exchange. The rules were established about confidentiality and trust. The men were allowed to share with each other without concern for being judged or belittled. The goal of the sharing is to establish a bond between the men as they disclose to each other. One of the primary lessons for men to learn in the mentoring process is the sacredness of a relationship, and the commitment one makes to a relationship. Many men have experienced difficulties in establishing healthy relationships with both men and women. Some men have experienced pain and disappointment from those with whom they ha e developed relationships in the past. Consequently, some men are skeptical or reluctant to establish new relationships. The writer used this information as a guide in developing the manual on mentoring.

Methods

A manual was developed to reflect those comments in the surveys of men in the church and community. Lessons were also developed to reflect the comments and suggestions of pastors surveyed. There were lessons taught from the manual to men in Bethany Baptist Church. There were 15 men agreeing to meet on Saturday mornings for five weekends. The men were taught two lessons each weekend, for a total of tell lessons from the manual. The men were encouraged to attend each meeting on time (8:00 a.m. to 10:00 a.m.). Breakfast food was served each morning the men met. It proved to be a powerful incentive for the men arriving on time, and also for regular attendance.

Research Design:

Fifty questionnaire forms (see appendix 5) along with the manual (see appendix 6) were developed for this protect and randomly mailed to pastors and lay-leaders throughout the United States. A self-addressed envelope was sent with the manual so that the surveys could be returned to the researcher once completed. There were a total of 34 completed questionnaires returned. Seventeen responses from pastors were returned, representing a 50% and sixteen from the lay-leaders representing 47%. There was an overwhelming 90% positive response from the pastors indicating that they would use the manual for mentoring training.

There were over 85% of the lay-leaders indicating that they would use the mentoring training manual.

Context

The Bethany Baptist Church is the context for this project. It is a church located on the west side of Detroit in a predominantly African American community. The community is comprised mostly of adults with high school education or less. The homes are mostly headed by females without husbands. The income is below poverty and is supplemented by the government issued. According to the 2000 census, the Bethany Baptist Church community is economically depressed. It is in this context that the men are called upon to become active mentors to other men and boys from this community in the community in which there is much deprivation. This community requires more than intervention, it requires divine intervention, and the church is equipped by God to meet the need. This writer believes that the church is called to make men after God's own image.

Participants

The participants in the project were initially African American men from the congregation at the Bethany Baptist Church. The men were informed by their pastor, Dr. Bullock what the training would entail and the men were asked to volunteer for the training. The men's ages varied from early twenties to eighty years of age. The men had different levels of education and experiences. One of the men was a retired Army non-commissioned officer. He knew how to train men and he was eager to get this training so that he could be helpful to the church. Several of the men were family men with children and grandchildren.

Most of these men had high school education or above, and were either employed or living off of their retirement income. Some of them were active leaders in the congregation.

Procedures

The first training of the mentors took place at Bethany Baptist Church. I requested and received permission from Dr. Bullock, the pastor to do the training with volunteers from the congregation. There were approximately twenty men starting the program by coming to the orientation meeting. After the first two meetings the group leveled off at fifteen men and it remained constant. The group consisted of men that committed to attending the remaining sessions. After the third meeting, the men agreed that the membership in the group was closed.

During the orientation meeting, the men were informed of the mentoring training process. They were given information that included the dates, times, and subjects that would be covered in each meeting. They were also given the format for each session (see the format in the manual, chapter 7). The men were asked to reflect on their lives and to think about those who had been their mentors. The responses were varied, emotional, and extremely informative to the writer and the other participants. One participant surprised the writer by identifying his mentor as one who had demonstrated negative mentoring. His insight was very impressive and helpful to the rest of us (he related how his father's mistakes had taught him how not to behave; negative mentoring). I never forgot to talk about negative mentoring after that event.

The men were given refreshments at the beginning of each session. Prayers were requested to be spoken by the elders in the group in each session. The elder was chosen to offer prayer so the men could begin to process the notion of mentors being sages. The writer always identified the elder in the group so that he could be validated, affirmed, and lifted up. The response from the elder for this recognition was amazing. They really liked the attention and the affirmations. The younger men also were eager to give the affirmations to the elders.

The participants were assigned specific scriptures for daily reading. They were told to read five chapters in the book of Psalms each day along with one Proverb each day. The entire book of Psalms and Proverbs could be covered in a month with this regimen of reading. The scriptures would be discussed briefly at the beginning of each class session.

The men were encouraged to choose a partner during each session, and they were encouraged to discuss the issues-concerns or celebrations that had occurred during the past week. The men's discussions occurred over a meal that was served each time they came together. The meal also served to encourage the men to arrive on time because it was ready when they arrived. The food was usually easy to prepare and inexpensive (muffins. sausages. fruit. juice. etc.).

The writer would always present the agenda for the session to let the men know what subjects would be covered. A review and summary of lessons completed were provided. Participants also were given additional reading assignments related to men issues and mentoring (see chapter 7).

Assessment

The first session would include a pre-test to determine what the men knew about mentoring. At the end of the sessions and the completion of the training, the men would be given a post-test so that I could determine their level of mastery of the material presented (after the training). The results gleaned from training these men prepared the writer to develop the mentoring manual.

Conclusions

The writer made an observation that there was a very noticeable disproportion of men to women in the Bethany Baptist church. The review of literature informed the writer that the disproportion of men to women in the church is a norm for many congregations.

The writer began asking men why they did not attend church using oral interviews and written surveys. The manual was developed in response to the needs expressed in the interviews and surveys.

Men were trained in the Bethany Baptist Church to become mentors to other men in the church and its community. The training emphasized the importance of having a relationship with God, and a relationship with others.

Men from the Bethany Baptist Church volunteered to become mentors through the training process, and agreed to become mentors to other men. After the training, they were presented certificates of completion before the congregation in a "laying on of hands" by the pastor during a Sunday morning worship service. The men were proud and the congregation was very affirming. It was very gratifying day for the men and the pastor. The results from this training provided the writer with information and skills for future training.

CHAPTER 5

Results

Men
Mentoring
Men

A Training Manual
By
Jerome P. Stevenson, Sr., LPCC, IBCC

Introduction

The purpose of this manual is to place a tool into the hands of persons who are serving as leaders in the community of faith so that they can train men to become mentors to other men. Mentoring is the preferred method of relating to men because it can address many of the issues impacting men in our culture. This biblical approach to mentoring will include male issues such as: spiritual, sexual, social, physical, and intellectual. The lessons in this manual have been treated in the field by two groups. The first treatment was a group of fifteen men at the Bethany Baptist Church of Detroit, Michigan. The second group was a group of men is the American Baptist Churches of Southeastern Michigan. These men were given pre-tests before the training, and a post-test after the training. The tests were given to determine the effectiveness of the lessons, and to measure the degree of learning that occurred among the participants.

This training can be divided into five sessions with each session consisting of five weeks. The demands of training require a commitment on the part of the leader and those seeking to become mentors. The lessons are presented in a building format. Each lesson is a prerequisite to the next. The knowledge gained from each lesson will enable the men to understand the future lessons better. Therefore, it is important for the participants to attend each week for a continuation and connection to previously taught lessons. The theme, "Iron Sharpens Iron", so one man sharpens another[80], will be focused throughout this manual. The theme represents the attempt of this manual to train men how to he intentionally connected to each other in a positive, effective, and spiritual relationship.

---

[80]   Proverbs 27:17. NIV

Objectives

Upon completion of this mentoring training, the participants will understand the purposes, practices and processes of mentoring. The participants will know the distinctions between secular and spiritual mentoring. The reading assignments in the Bible are given to the men so that they can enhance their relationship with God through the reading of Psalms, and enhance their relationship with each other through the reading of the Proverbs. Each time the mentor and mentoree come together, they can discuss the Proverbs and the Psalms.

To demonstrate competency in this mentoring training, the participants will be able to accomplish the following tasks:

- Define the word mentor as it relates to secular and spiritual contexts.
- Describe the continuation of mentoring in the spiritual context.
- Identify mentors in the Old and New Testament.
- They will be able to explain how Deuteronomy 6:1-10 is related to mentoring.
- Describe the origin of mentoring in the Bible and secular history.
- Identify essential characteristics of mentors.
- Explain how mentoring differs from discipleship.

Pretest

The pretest is given as a formative evaluation of the lessons. The test will reveal the level of knowledge men have prior to the training that can be compared to a summative evaluation in a post-test after the training, to determine the level of comprehension and competency.

1. **From your present knowledge and experience, give the meaning of the word "mentor" as it relates to the secular context.**

   _____

   _____

   _____

2. **From your present knowledge and experience, give the meaning of the word "mentor" as it relates to the spiritual context.**

   _____

   _____

   _____

3. **Give one reason why "mentoring" is important in the work place.**

   _____

   _____

   _____

4. **Give one reason why "mentoring" is important in the place of worship.**

   _____

   _____

   _____

5. Who was the primary "mentor" in the Old Testament?

_____

_____

_____

6. Who was the primary "mentor" in the New Testament?

_____

_____

_____

7. What are some essential characteristics of a mentor?

_____

_____

_____

_____

_____

_____

Answers: see appendix one
(The pretest is given for evaluation purposes)

Lesson Procedure and Format

Who is the mentoring group leader/trainer?
The group leader trainer can be anyone who has received this training course, or someone who is a leader with training experience. Ideally, the leader trainer would be the pastor, ministerial staff, or a lay leader.

What happens when men meet?
Each time the men gather, they will be encouraged to share their concerns (death, sickness, job loss, demotion, etc.) and celebrations (birth, promotion, marriage, birthday, anniversary, etc.) while enjoying refreshments. The leader can bless the refreshments or ask an elder to bless it. The leader should ask an elder within the group to offer prayer based upon what has been shared and celebrated during the meal. After each session, the leader will ask an elder member of the group to close with prayer.

The leader introduces and explains the topic for each session with goals and objectives.
After the leader has made the assignment for the session, the men will gather in groups of four to six men and select a recorder and reporter. The recorder will take notes of the discussion and share them with the reporter. The reporter will share notes of the small group discussion with the larger group that is reassembled by the leader. The group will meet for fifteen to twenty minutes on each topic and reassemble for discussion in the larger group. After each group discussion, the leader will summarize the lesson, and repeat the lesson objective.

How often do men meet?
The mentoring program training can consist of twenty-five weeks sessions. The trainer should survey the men to determine the best time of year to begin the training.

The suggested time schedule for each meeting is as follows (2 hours):

Arrival and Prayer	(10 minutes)
Refreshments and Sharing	(20 minutes)
Lesson Introduction and Instruction	(15 minutes)
Small Group Discussion	(20 minutes)
Larger Group Discussion	(20 minutes)
Reading Assignment	(10 minutes)
Prayer/Dismissal	(10 minutes)

When do the men meet?

The training can be taught on Saturdays or Sunday Mornings during the Sunday School hour. Practice has shown that men will attend with more regularity and enthusiasm if they are given refreshments at each session.

Why do the men meet?

The men should meet each week to learn lessons that cover the principles, practices and processes of mentoring. The lessons cover topics that will be discussed in small and large group settings. The small groups will have a recorder to take notes of the discussion, and a reporter who will share the notes with the larger group once reassembled by the leader.

Where do the men meet?

The place where men meet should be secure enough to foster confidentiality, large enough for group breakouts, and located close enough for the participants to travel a reasonable distance. Men sitting at large tables of four each is an ideal arrangement; the tables should he far enough apart so that conversations will be isolated between groups. Round tables are preferred if available.

Schedule and Outline of Training

Session 1: Mentoring and its Beginnings.
- **A.** God used mentoring to nurture, instruct, model, and to show courage.
- **B.** Mentoring in Secular History.
- **C.** Mentoring in creation.
- **D.** God used mentoring to teach man his attributes.

Session 2: Mentoring in the Old Testament
- **A.** Mentoring and God.
- **B.** Mentoring and Moses.
- **C.** Mentoring by the elders.
- **D** Mentoring as a relationship and commitment.
- **E.** Mentoring and accountability.

Session 3: Mentoring in the New Testament
- **A.** Mentoring as a calling.
- **B.** Mentoring and discipleship.
- **C.** Mentoring and evangelism.
- **D.** Mentoring and the gospel.
- **E.** Mentoring in the Early Church.

Session 4: Mentoring in Culture
- **A.** Mentoring and its origin.
- **B.** Mentoring in academia.
- **C.** Mentoring and the work place.
- **D.** Mentoring and communication.
- **F.** Mentoring and relationships.

Session 5: Mentoring in Context
- **A.** Mentoring as a witness.
- **B.** Mentoring as discipleship.
- **C.** Mentoring and evangelism.
- **D.** Mentoring as a skill.
- **E.** Mentoring Post-test Evaluation.

Session One

(This session is chosen first to familiarize the participants with the new terms and the process for mentoring)

Lesson one (week one)

Mentoring Lessons Objectives:

    A. What is the purpose of (nurture) in mentoring?
    B. Why is (instruction) used in mentoring?
    C. How is (modeling) done in mentoring?
    D. Where is (courage) appropriate in mentoring?

Procedure:

Every lesson should be preceded with prayer and refreshments. The men are encouraged to share concerns and celebrations at each meeting during the meal. Mentoring is a relational process, and men should engage each other as often as possible to enhance the relationship. Concerns could be personal problems or challenges i.e. (death, sickness, divorce, demotion, job loss, etc.) Celebrations could be those happy events in one's life i.e. (birthday, anniversary, fatherhood, promotions, etc.)

After the group has shared concerns and celebrations the leader should introduce the next lesson.

Lesson Ice Breaker:

Ask the men to read some verses of Proverbs Chapter One and discuss it while eating. The leader will ask someone to read the following scripture for lesson discussion.

Deuteronomy 6:1-10

[1]These are the commands, decrees and laws the Lord your God directed me to teach you to observe in the land that you are

crossing the Jordan to possess, [2]so that you, your children and their children after them may fear the Lord your God as long as you live by keeping all his decrees and commands that I give you, and so that you may enjoy long life. [3]Hear, O Israel, and be careful to obey so that it may go well with you and that you may increase greatly in a land flowing with milk and honey, just as the Lord the God of your fathers, promised you. [4]Hear, O Israel: The Lord our God, the Lord is one. [5]Love the Lord your God with all your heart and with all your soul and with all your strength. [6]These commandments that I give you today are to be upon your hearts. [7]Impress them on your children. Talk about them when you sit at home and when you walk along the road, when you lie down and when you get up. [8]Tie them as symbols on your hands and bind them on your foreheads. [9]Write them on the doorframes of your houses and on your gates. [10]When the Lord your God brings you into the land he swore to our fathers, to Abraham, Isaac and Jacob, to give you a land with large, flourishing cities you did not build.

In the above Scripture, mentoring was used by God to instruct, nurture, guide, and to bless the Israelites, the people of God. They were told to obey God's commands so that His commands could be learned and continued by the Israelites from one generation to another. The method, by which the Israelites could continue the teaching, was mentoring. Each generation mentored the next.

Small group discussion:

The recorder will write down the comments and opinions of the group participants. The reporter will share what was discussed in the small group to the larger group. The leader will ask the men to gather in small groups of four or six to discuss these terms below and revisit the Scripture above (Deuteronomy 6:1–10) for a connection. These terms are defined later in this lesson below.

- *Nurturing*
- *Instruct*
- *Model*
- *Encourage*

Large Group discussion:

The mentor leader will lead the larger group discussion about the terms assigned and close the discussion with a definition for each term:

o <u>Nurturing</u> – To rear; bring up; training; education.[81]
o <u>Instruct</u> – To give knowledge to; show how to do; teach; train; educate.[82]
o <u>Model</u> – Figurative; A thing or person to be copied or imitated; exemplar.[83]
o <u>Encourage</u> – to give hope, or confidence to; urge on.[84]

The leader should summarize the lesson by reviewing the terms covered and repeating the definitions.

Reading Assignment:

Proverb for each day of the week
Read five Psalms per day in each week

---

[81]   *The World Book Dictionary* (1987), s.v. "nurture."
[82]   Ibid., s.v. "instruct."
[83]   Ibid., s.v. "model."
[84]   Ibid., s.v. "encourage."

Lesson two (week two)

Procedure:

Every lesson should be preceded with prayer and refreshments. The men are encouraged to share concerns and celebrations at each meeting during the meal. Mentoring is a relational process, and men should engage each other as often as possible to enhance the relationship. Concerns could be personal problems or challenges i.e. (death, sickness, divorce, demotion, job loss, etc.) Celebrations could be those happy events in one's life i.e. (birthday, anniversary, fatherhood, promotions, etc.)

After the group has shared concerns and celebrations, the leader should introduce the next lesson.

Lesson Ice Breaker:

Ask the men to read some verses of Proverbs Chapter Two and discuss it while eating. The leader will ask someone to read the following scripture for lesson discussion.

Lesson Objective:

Men will learn why Mentoring is used according to secular history. The group leader will lecture on the purposes of mentoring to the men prior to them assembling in a small group discussion; the leader will say to the men that mentoring has been used effectively to pass on important information from one generation to another throughout history. Secular history records the beginning of mentoring in Greek Mythology. Its origin can be traced back to Homer's Greek classic, *The Odyssey*. Mentor was the name of the character that was hired by Ulysses to teach his son while he was away at war. Mentor was hired to nurture, instruct, model, and encourage the son of Ulysses.

Daloz, in his book, "Mentor" gives us some history on the term as it was used historically and in our contemporary culture:

Although, mentors have always been around, in the years since Gail Sheehy popularized the term (in *Passages*, 1976) mentors have become increasingly visible. Success, we are told whether in industry or academia is a lot slippier without a mentor to show us the ropes. A flood of books and articles now proclaim mentors' virtues and defects (Speizer, 1981 Merriam, 1983; Gray, 1989; Bey and Holmes, 1992; Cohen, 1995; Luna and Cullen, 1997: Waters, 1998). And who has not read *Tuesday with Morrie* (Albomt, 1997), that bittersweet journal of a young man and his dying mentor?

Yet, relatively little work has been done on the deeper, metaphorical and archetypal context of the word. As we will see in a moment, it is of more than passing interest that the original mentor as inhabited by Athena. Clearly, the mentor is concerned with transmission of wisdom. How, then, do mentors transmit wisdom? Most often, it seems, they take us on a journey. In this aspect of their work, mentors are guides. They lead us along the journey of our lives. We trust them because they have been there before. They embody our hopes, cast light on the way ahead, interpret arcane signs, warn us of lurking dangers, and point out unexpected delights along the way. There is certain luminosity about them, and they often pose as magicians in tales of transformation, for *magic* is a word given to what we cannot see and we can rarely see across the gulf. As teachers of adults, we have much to learn from the mythology of the mentor.[85]

In the quote above, Daloz mentions the book written by Mitch Albom, a famous sports writer, and his college professor, who was his mentor. The significance of the story is that Mitch did not realize how appreciative his professor was for him to acknowledge

---

[85] Laurent A. Daloz, *Mentor* (San Francisco: Jossey-Bass Publishers, 1999), 18-19.

the value of his professor to him as a mentor. Mitch's disclosure was very precious to the professor especially as his life was coming to a close. Often, we fail to let others know the important contributions they have made in our development as humans. The sharing of these stories is helpful to both the mentor and the mentoree.

Spiritual mentoring was common in the eighteenth century as pastors allowed disciples to reside in their homes to learn and observe the quality of marriage and personal spiritual dynamics. Sadly, mentoring has become a lost art even in the church. We inherited the perfect model for mentoring in Jesus Christ. His twelve disciples were able to carry on a ministry that turned the world upside down, and were responsible for the New Testament Church that has a legacy to this day. This manual is an attempt to recapture those mentoring paradigms found in the Scriptures. The Bible is replete with examples of effective mentoring:

Jethro mentored Moses, Moses mentored Joshua, Naomi mentored Ruth, Elijah mentored Elisha, Elizabeth mentored Mary, Jesus mentored the disciples, Barnabas mentored Paul, Paul mentored Timothy and Titus, and Priscilla and Aquila mentored Apollos. There are many churches with multiple staff members who are mentored by senior staff and the pastor.

Sellner gives the following history of mentoring in our Christian history:

> **The Spiritual Mentor in the Christian Tradition**:
> The rich tradition of spiritual mentoring in Christianity clearly transcends differences in personality, sex, age and culture.
>
> From the desert tradition we are given Anthony and Pachomiu, pioneers in Christian Asceticism, who reminds us that spirituality demands discipline. From Ireland the Christian Shaman Columcille tells us that sometimes we may feel like exiles in our search for God. Twelfth-century English Cistercian Aelred of Rievaulx counsels us on the joys of spiritual friendship,

and the 14th Century mystic Julian of Norwich assures us that all will be well. From Germany, Meister Eckhart speaks of creation and the awe fundamental to Christian living. From Greece Gregory Palamas teaches us to pray continuously from the heart. From Italy come the two Catherines, of Genoa and Siena; the first describes the immense love of God, and the second reminds us that even church authorities may need to be challenged to accept ongoing reform. From Spain Ignatius guides us in the discernment of spirits, and Teresa and John gives us directions in interior castles and dark nights of the soul.

Wise pastors of the Protestant tradition such as Luther, Zwingli and Calvin speak of the priesthood of all believers, the need for ministry to include all sorts of people, lay and ordained, women and men, single and married. Bunyan, Fox and Wesley remind us that grace abounds and life is a pilgrimage that we need to pay more attention to the inner light, that confession is good for the soul. And in more recent times the Anglican converts Evelyn Underhill and C. S. Lewis share with us mystics and myths, adult stories for children and children's stories for adults, while Thomas Merton and Dorothy Day confront us with the need to relate prayer and social justice.[86]

Given the influence, significance and the power of mentoring, it is essential that the places of worship employ this process to reach and meet the needs of men in their places of worship and community.

Reading Assignment:

Proverb chapter 1
First five chapters of Psalms

---

[86] Edward C. Sellner, *Mentoring The Ministry of Spiritual Kinship* (Notre Dame: Ave Maria Press, 1990), 32-33.

Lesson three (week three)

Mentoring in Creation

Then God said, "Let Us make man in Our image, according to Our likeness ..."[87]

Lesson Objectives:

- Men will learn what it means to be made in the image of God.
- Men will learn what it means to be made in the likeness of God.
- Men will learn what it means to have a mentoring image.
- Men will learn what it means to have a mentoring likeness.
- Men will learn what it means to multiply and not duplicate themselves.

Procedure:

Every lesson should be preceded with prayer and refreshments. The men are encouraged to share concerns and celebrations at each meeting. The purpose of the sharing during each lesson is to prepare the men to become routine in their concern and care for each other. The more they practice sharing and caring the more it will become a routine.

The main focus of mentoring is relationship and relationship building. Relationships will be the adhesive that keep the men bonded and accountable to one another.

The leader should review these principles as often as the opportunity permits. The more the men hear the principles of having significant relationships, the more they will respect and strive to build good and healthy relationships.

---

[87]   Genesis 1:26. NIV

Session one will be the format to follow for each lesson. The leader should continue to refer to the lessons in session one so that the routines of the remaining lessons will be adhered to without deviation.

The men will gather in groups of four or six to discuss the meaning of being made in the image of God.[88] The group will assign someone to be a recorder and also someone to be a reporter. These guides apply whenever groups are formed. The leader should allow the groups to dialogue 10–15 minutes each session and break to a larger group.

After the group has shared concerns and celebrations, the leader should introduce the next lesson.

Lesson Ice Breaker:

Ask the men to read some verses of Proverbs three and discuss it while eating.

1. The men will use the Bible to look up the scripture; Genesis 1:26.
2. The men will discuss what the scripture means by image? **Note:** If the men get stuck on *image*, the leader can suggest that the men talk about the attributes of God.

Answer: The Holman Bible Dictionary image as follows:

Image

The Hebrew ***selem*** or image refers to a hewn or carved image[89] like a statue, which bears a strong physical resemblance to the person or thing it represents.

---

[88] Genesis 1:26. NIV
[89] 1 Samuel 6:5; 2 Kings 11:18. NIV

Likeness

The word *likeness, demuth*, means a facsimile. Compare 2 Kings 16:10, "fashion" or "pattern" (NASB), "sketch" (NIV, REB), and "exact model" (TEV). Neither of the words implies that persons are divine. They were endowed with some of the characteristics of God. There is a likeness, but not sameness.

Reading Assignment:

Proverb each day of the week
Five Psalms each day of the week

Lesson four (week four)

Procedure:

Every lesson should be preceded with prayer and refreshments. The men are encouraged to share concerns and celebrations at each meeting.

After the group has shared concerns and celebrations, the leader should introduce the next lesson.

Lesson Ice Breaker:

Ask the men to read some verses of Proverbs four and discuss it while eating.

Topic Discussion:

Humans can have similar attributes of God such as:

- Grace
- Love
- Kindness
- Goodness
- Truth

Objectives

- Men will learn the meaning of God's Grace.
- Men will learn the meaning of God's Love.
- Men will learn the meaning of God's Kindness.
- Men will learn the meaning of God's Goodness.
- Men will learn the meaning of God's Truth.

The leader will assign the men to groups of four or six. They will select a reporter and a recorder for the group. The group will read and discuss the following definitions regarding the attributes of God:

GRACE   Undeserved acceptance and love received from another, especially the characteristic attitude of God in providing salvation for sinners. For Christians, the word "grace" is virtually synonymous with the gospel of God's gift of unmerited salvation in Jesus Christ. To express this, the New Testament writers used the Greek word *charis*, which had a long previous history in secular Greek. Related to the word for joy or pleasure, *charis* originally referred to something delightful or attractive in a person, something which brought pleasure to others. From this it came to have the idea of a favor or kindness done to another or of a gift, which brought pleasure to another. Viewed from the standpoint of the recipient, it was used to refer to the thankfulness felt for a gift or favor. These meanings also appear in the biblical use of *charis,* but only in the New Testament does it come to have the familiar sense which grace bears for Christians.[90]

LOVE   Unselfish, loyal, and benevolent concern for the wellbeing of another. In I Corinthians 13, Paul described "love" as a more excellent way than tongues or even preaching. The New Testament maintains this estimation of love throughout. The King James Version uses the word charity instead of "love" to translate the Greek word Paul used *(agape).* The word charity comes from the Latin *caritas,* which means "dearness" "affection", or "high regard." Today, the word *charity* is normally used for acts of benevolence, and so the word love is to be preferred as a translation of *agape.* Nevertheless, the reader who comes to the *agape* of the New Testament with the idea of benevolence in mind is better off than the reader who comes with the idea of physical pleasure and satisfaction.[91]

---

[90]   Holman Dictionary, Quickverse
[91]   Ibid.

KINDNESS   The steadfast love that maintains relationships through gracious aid in times of need.

Old Testament The principal word used to express kindness in the Old Testament (*chesed*) bears the connotation of a loyal love, which manifests itself not in emotions but in actions. Originally, this loving kindness was considered an integral part of covenant relations. It was reciprocal and expected, a deed performed in return for a previous loyalty. Rahab expected kindness in return for her kindness to the spies (Josh. 2:12. 14). Joseph expected kindness from the cupbearer in return for the interpretation of a dream (Gen. 40:14). In this sense, kindness was distinct from mercy or compassion, which was more of an emotion and from grace which was not as closely associated with covenant keeping. In time, however, the concepts of kindness, mercy, and grace intermingled.

Kindness was shown in social relationships as the bond between host and guest (Gen. 19:19), ruler and subject (2 Sam. 16:17), or friends (1 Sam. 20:8). It was the faithfulness expected of a good person (Prov. 3:3). Primarily, kindness characterized the covenant relation between God and his people. God's faithful love accompanied the patriarchs and dwelt with those who kept His covenant (Gen. 24:27: Ex. 20:6). The Psalms developed this theme with thanksgiving for divine kindness and praise for its endurance (Ps. 86:5; 89:2, 28; 100:5; 103:8, 11, 17; 106:1; 107:1; etc.; see especially Ps. 136). Slow to anger and abounding in love became a characteristic description of Israel's Lord, distinguishing His kindness from His wrath (Ex. 34:6; Num. 14:18; Neh. 9:17; Ps. 103:8; 145:8; Jonah 4:2; Joel 2:13).

Human response to the covenant with God, however, was bewailed by the prophets as a youthful loyalty that vanished like the morning dew (Jer. 2:2; Hos. 6:4). In this situation God's kindness always has an aspect of freedom (Ex. 33:19) and mingles with mercy and grace. It is an everlasting love which cannot be shaken (Isa. 54:8, 10).

New Testament Although both use of humankind (Acts 28:2) and brotherly love (2 Pet.1:7) are translated as kindness in the New Testament, the Greek word bearing the richest connotation is *chrestotes* (kras totas). This word has a basic meaning of usefulness and is translated as goodness, gentleness, and kindness. Once again, actions are emphasized, especially God's gracious actions toward sinners (Titus 3:4; Rom. 11:22). The kindness God has shown us through Christ is equivalent to his grace and embodies the fullness of salvation (Eph. 2:7). When kindness is included in lists of human virtues, it can be understood as helpfulness to others prompted by an experience of God's redemptive love (2 Cor. 6:6; Gal. 5:22; Col. 3:12).[92]

Barbara J. Bruce

GOOD   In contrast to the Greek view of "the good" as an idea, the biblical concept focuses on concrete experiences of what God has done and is doing in the lives of God's people. Scripture affirms that God is and does good (1 Chron. 16:34; Ps. 119:68). The goodness of God is experienced in the goodness of God's creative work (Gen. 1:31) and in God's saving acts (liberation of Israel from Egypt, Ex. 18:9; return of a remnant from captivity, Ezra 7:9; personal deliverance, Ps. 34:8; salvation, Phil. 1:6). God's goodness is extended to God's name (Ps. 52:9), God's promises (Jos. 21:45), God's commands (Ps. 119:39; Rom. 7:12), God's gifts (Jas. 1:17), and God's providential shaping of events (Gen. 50:20; Rom. 8:28). Though God alone is truly good (Ps.14:1, 3; Mark 10:18). Scripture repeatedly speaks of good persons who seek to live their lives in accordance with God's will. Christians have been saved in order to do good (Eph. 2:10; Col. 1:10) with the Holy Spirit's help.[93]

---

[92]   Ibid.
[93]   Ibid.

TRUTH   That which is reliable and can be trusted, the Bible uses *truth* in the general "factual" sense. Truth may designate the actual fact over against appearance, pretense, or assertion. In Zechariah 8:16 (NRSV) the Lord of hosts declared: "These are the things that you shall do: Speak the truth to one another, render in your gates judgments that are true and make for peace." When Jesus asked, "Who touched my garments?" the woman who had been healed through touching Jesus' garments fell down before him, and told him all the truth (Mark 5:32-33). In 1 and 2 Timothy, truth is correct knowledge or doctrine. Certain individuals had departed from proper doctrine. Some "forbid marriage and demand abstinence from foods, which God created to be received with thanksgiving by those who believe and know the truth" (1Tim. 4:3 NRSV). Some have "swerved from the truth by claiming that the resurrection has already taken place (2 Tim. 2:18 NRSV).[94]

Reassemble

The group leader will reassemble the men for the large group discussion based upon the notes of the recorder. The reporter from each group will share with the larger group.

The leader will allow questions and answers based upon the reports from the groups.

The leader will summarize the objectives learned and emphasize key concepts from the discussion.

Reading Assignment:

Proverb each day of the week
Five Psalms each day of the week

---

[94]   Ibid.

Objective:

Proverbs gives us wisdom about our horizontal relationship with each other.

Psalms gives us wisdom about our vertical relationship with God.

Lesson five (week five)

Lesson Objectives:
- Men will learn how mentors can have god-like attributes.
- Men will learn how mentors can have godly thoughts.
- Men will learn how mentors can have god-like analysis.
- Men will learn that mentors can have the spirit of God.

Humans can be like God by
- Thinking
- Analyzing
- Having a spirit

- **Mentioning Image**
  Mentoring image means that a mentor has a life that can he mirrored by the mentoree. The following qualities are necessary:

- **The mentor is holy in lifestyle**
  1 Peter 1:16
  "for it is written: "Be holy, because I am holy.""

- **The mentor is particular about the company he keeps.**
  Psalm 1:1
  "Blessed is the man who does not walk in the counsel of the wicked or stand in the way of sinners or sit in the seat of mockers.""

- **The mentor is spiritual**
  Romans 8:14
  "because those who are led by the Spirit of God are sons of God.""

- **The mentor is relational and is not afraid to display love.**
  John 13:34
  "A new command I give you: Love one another. As I have loved you, so you must love one another."

- **The mentor is open and accepting of the mentoree**
  Romans 15:7
  "Accept one another, then, just as Christ accepted you, in order to bring praise to God."

- **The mentor is compassionate with the mentoree**
  Ephesians 4:32
  "Be kind and compassionate to one another, forgiving each other, just as in Christ God forgave you."

Mentoring Likeness:

- **The mentor is role model to the mentoree**
  Philippians 4:9
  "Whatever you have learned or received or heard from me, or seen in me put it into practice. And the God of peace will be with you."

Philippians 3:17 (NIV)

Join with others in following my example, brothers, and take note of those who live according to the pattern we gave you,

- **The mentor is able to multiply himself through the mentoree**
  Mentoring is not about duplication, it is at its best when multiplication takes place. Each mentoree has his own set of skills and gifts that are uniquely given to him by God. The mentor simply journeys with the mentoree coaching

and encouraging the mentoree to develop and use his gifts to the glory of God.

Proverbs 18:16 (NAS)

A man's gift makes room for him, and brings him before great men.

The group leader will reassemble the men and ask the group reporter to share the highlights of the small group discussion that were written by the recorder.

The leader can encourage the men to ask questions about the lesson and objectives learned.

Note: The above lesson is to be taught over a period of five weeks. The weeks should include assigned readings.

A suggested reading follows:

Mentor by Laurent A. Daloz
Mentoring The Ministry of Spiritual Kinship by Edward C. Sellner
Tuesday with Morrie by Mitch Albom

Session Two

Mentoring in the Old Testament

Lesson one (week one)

Iron sharpens iron, so one man sharpens another (Proverbs 27:17).

Procedure:

Every lesson should be preceded with prayer and refreshments. The men are encouraged to share concerns and celebrations at each meeting.

After the group has shared concerns and celebrations, the leader should introduce the next lesson.

Lesson Ice Breaker:

Ask the men to read a few verses from Proverbs two for a discussion as they eat their refreshments.

Lesson Objectives:

- Men will learn why Jethro was considered a mentor.
- Men will learn why Moses was considered a leader.
- Men will learn how Moses mentored Joshua.
- Men will learn how Eli Mentored Samuel.
- Men will learn how Elijah mentored Elisha.

Introduction of lesson by the leader:

The leader can introduce this lesson by having the men to rethink about those mentors in their lives. Allow time for a few men to tell their mentoring stories.

Use this opportunity to share with the men, Biblical stories where men have mentored other men.

Assign the men to groups of four or six. They should select a reporter and a recorder. The recorder will take notes of the session and the reporter will share the notes with the larger group when the men reassemble after fifteen minutes breakout.

Lesson discussion small group:

Moses mentored by Jethro

The men will select someone to read the Scripture below. After the Scripture is read, the men should discuss the events and the counsel given by Jethro, Moses father-in-law. The men should discuss the importance of counsel by a mentor, and the role of the mentoree after receiving the counsel. Ask the men if they have always responded to wise counsel. What were the results?

Exodus 18:13-18 (NIV)

The next day Moses took his seat to serve as judge for the people, and they stood around him from morning till evening. When his father-in-law saw all that Moses was doing for the people, he said, "What is this you are doing for the people? Why do you alone sit as judge, while all these people stand around you from morning till evening?" Moses answered him, "Because the people come to me to seek God's will. Whenever they have a dispute, it is brought to me, and I decide between the parties and inform them of God's decrees and laws." Moses' father-in-law replied, "What you are doing is not good. You and these people who come to you will only wear yourselves out. The work is too heavy for you; you cannot handle it alone.

The leader will reassemble the men and use the group to discuss the mentoring incidents according the scriptural text assigned.

Each group reporter will share the highlights of the small group discussion with the larger group.

Reading Assignment:

Proverb each day this of the week

Five Psalms each day of the week

Objective:

Proverbs gives us wisdom about our horizontal relationship with each other.

Psalms gives us wisdom about our vertical relationship with God.

Lesson two (week two)

Mentoring in the Old Testament

Procedure:

Every lesson should be preceded with prayer and refreshments. The men are encouraged to share concerns and celebrations at each meeting.

After the group has shared concerns and celebrations, the leader will introduce the next lesson.

Lesson Ice Breaker:

Ask the men to read a few verses from Proverbs according to the date for a discussion as they eat their refreshments.

Lesson Objectives:

- Men will learn how Moses chose Joshua as a mentoree.
- Men will learn how Moses mentored Joshua.
- Men will learn why Moses mentored Joshua.
- Men will learn the results of Moses' mentoring to Joshua.

Moses mentored Joshua
Exodus 24:13 (week two)

Then Moses set out with Joshua his aide and Moses went up on the mountain of God. He said to the elders. "Wait here for us until we come back to you. Aaron and Hur are with you, and anyone involved in a dispute can go to them."

Deuteronomy 34:9 (NIV)

Now Joshua son of Nun was filled with the spirit of wisdom because Moses had laid his hands on him. So the Israelites listened to him and did what the LORD had commanded Moses. Joshua eventually became the leader of the Israelites after the death of

Moses. God assured Joshua that He would be with him as He was with Moses.

Joshua 1:5 (NIV)

No one will be able to stand up against you all the days of your life. As I was with Moses, so I will be with you; I will never leave you nor forsake you.

The leader will reassemble the men and use the group to discuss the mentoring incidents according the scriptural text assigned.

Each group reporter will share the highlights of the small group discussion with the larger group.

Leader:

Encourage the men to notice how Joshua was patient in the role of following before he began leading. The mentor's role is to lead, and the mentoree role is to follow.

Reading Assignment:

Proverb each day of the week (class discussion)
Five Psalms each day of the week (daily devotion)
The book of Samuel for next week's lesson

Note:

Proverbs gives us wisdom about our horizontal relationship with each other.
Psalms gives us wisdom about our vertical relationship with God.

Lesson three (week three)

Mentoring in the Old Testament

Procedure:

Every lesson should be preceded with prayer and refreshments. The men are encouraged to share concerns and celebrations at each meeting.

After the group has shared concerns and celebrations, the leader should introduce the next lesson.

Lesson Ice Breaker:

Ask the men to read a few verses from Proverbs according to the date for a discussion as they eat their refreshments.

Lesson Objective:

- Men will learn how older men can mentor to younger men.
- Men will learn the value of ageing and learning.
- Men will learn how wisdom and old age go together.

Eli mentored Samuel

Ask one of the men to read the scripture below. After reading the scripture, ask them to discuss their own relationship with older men. What attributes do older men have that are unique and valuable?

1 Samuel 3:1

The boy Samuel ministered before the Lord under Eli. In those days the word of the Lord was rare; there were not many visions. One night Eli, whose eyes were becoming so weak that he could barely see was lying down in his usual place. The lamp of God had not yet gone out, and Samuel was lying down in the temple of the Lord, where the ark of God was. Then the Lord called

Samuel. Samuel answered. Here I am." And he ran to Eli and said. "Here I am: you called me." But Eli said, I did not call; go back and lie down. So he went and lay down. Again the Lord called, Samuel! And Samuel got up and went to Eli and said. Here I am; you called me." "My son," Eli said. "I did not call; go back and lie down." Now Samuel did not yet know the Lord: The word of the Lord had not yet been revealed to him. The Lord called Samuel a third time and Samuel got up and went to Eli and said. "Here I am; you called me." Then Eli realized that the Lord was calling the boy. So Eli told Samuel. "Go and lie down, and he calls you say, Speak Lord for your servant is listening. So Samuel went and lay down in his place.

The leader will assign the men to groups of four or six for discussion about the mentoring event in the scripture. They are to discuss the process of mentoring between Eli and Samuel.

A recorder is assigned to make note about the discussion which are to be given to the reporter once completed.

Each group reporter will share the highlights of the small group discussion with the larger group.

The leader will reassemble the men and use the group to discuss the mentoring incidents according the scriptural text assigned.

The leader can ask the men to discuss Eli's position in the story, and how that position allowed him to become a mentor. How did Eli's position influence Samuel? What happened when Samuel obeyed Eli about his encounter with God?

Reading Assignment:

Proverb each day of the week (class discussion)
Five Psalms each day of the week (daily devotion) 1& 2 kings
From Age-ing to Sage-ing by Zalman Schachter-Shalomi Age-lug to Sage-ing by Zalman Schachter-Shalomi

Note:

Proverbs gives us wisdom about our horizontal relationship with each other.

Psalms gives us wisdom about our vertical relationship with God.

Lesson four (week four)

Mentoring in the Old Testament

Procedure:

Every lesson should be preceded with prayer and refreshments. The men are encouraged to share concerns and celebrations at each meeting.

After the group has shared concerns and celebrations, the leader should introduce the next lesson.

Lesson Ice Breaker:

Ask the men to read a few verses from Proverbs according to the date for a discussion as they eat their refreshments.

Elijah mentored Elisha Lesson Objective:

- Men will learn about the commitment of mentoring.
- Men will learn about the mentoring relationship.
- Men will learn about the sacrifice of mentoring.
- Men will learn about the advantages of mentoring.

Leader: Have one of the men to read the Scripture below

I Kings 19:19 (NIV)

So Elijah went from there and found Elisha son of Shaphat, he was plowing with twelve yoke of oxen, and he himself was driving the twelfth pair. Elijah went up to him and threw his cloak around him. Elisha then left his oxen and ran after Elijah. Let me kiss my father and mother good-by," he said, "and then I will come with you." "Go back." Elijah replied. "What have I done to you?" So Elisha left him and went back. He took his yoke of oxen and slaughtered them. He burned the plowing equipment to cook the meat and gave it to the people and they ate. Then he set out to follow Elijah and became his attendant.

Have the men to discuss the sequence of events that led to Elijah actually choosing Elisha, his mentoree. The commitment to Elisha by Elijah was convincing enough so that Elisha destroyed the instruments of his lively hood and followed Elijah. Have the men to discuss the meaning of one man's commitment to another.

The leader will assign the men to groups of four or six for discussion about the mentoring event in the scripture. They are to discuss the process of mentoring between Eli and Samuel.

A recorder is assigned to make note about the discussion which are to be given to the reporter once completed.

The leader will reassemble the men and use the group to discuss the mentoring incidents according the scriptural text assigned.

Each group reporter will share the highlights of the small group discussion with the larger group.

The leader will lead the large group discussion after the reports have been shared to determine if the men have understood the objectives.

Questions to ask:

- What was Elisha doing when he was called to the ministry?
- How do you know Elisha made a total commitment to the call?
- What was Elijah's approach to Elisha in the call to ministry?
- What roll did Elisha assume with Elijah?
- What was the outcome of Elisha as a mentoree of Elijah?

Reading Assignment:

Proverb each day of the week (class discussion)
Five Psalms each day of the week (daily devotion)

2 Samuel 7-12

From Age-ing to Sage-ing by Zalman Schachter–Shalomi
(continue reading)

Note:

Proverbs gives us wisdom about our horizontal relationship with each other.

Psalms gives us wisdom about our vertical relationship with God.

Lesson five (week five)

Mentoring in the Old Testament

Procedure:

Every lesson should be preceded with prayer and refreshments. The men are encouraged to share concerns and celebrations at each meeting.

After the group has shared concerns and celebrations, the leader should introduce the next lesson.

Lesson ice Breaker:

Ask the men to read a few verses from Proverbs according to the date for a discussion as they eat their refreshments.

Lesson Introduction: Nathan mentors David, the king

The leader will ask one of the men to read 2 Samuel 7:1-17; 11-12

2 Samuel 7:1 (NIV)

[1]After the king was settled in his palace and the Lord had given him rest from all his enemies around him, he said to Nathan the prophet, "Here I am, living in a house of cedar, while the ark of God remains in a tent." Nathan replied to the king, "Whatever you have in mind, go ahead and do it, for the Lord is with you." But that night the word of the Lord came to Nathan, saying: "Go and tell my servant David, 'This is what the Lord says: Are you the one to build me a house to dwell in? I have not dwelt in a house from the day I brought the Israelites up out of Egypt to this day. I have been moving from place to place with a tent as my dwelling. Wherever I have moved with all the Israelites, did I ever say to any of their rulers whom I commanded to shepherd my people Israel, "Why have you not built me a house of cedar?" "Now then, tell my servant, David. 'This is what the Lord Almighty says: I took

you from the pasture, from tending the flock, and appointed you ruler over my people Israel. I have been with you wherever you have gone, and I have cut off all your enemies from before you. Now I will make your name great, like the names of the greatest men on earth. And I will provide a place for my people Israel and will plant them so that they can have a home of their own and no longer be disturbed. Wicked people will not oppress them anymore, as they did at the beginning and have done ever since the time I appointed leaders over my people Israel. I will also give you rest from all your enemies.

"'The Lord declares to you that the Lord himself will establish a house for you. When your days are over and you rest with your ancestors, I will raise up your offspring to succeed you, your own flesh and blood, and I will establish his kingdom. He is the one who will build a house for my Name, and I will establish the throne of his kingdom forever. I will be his father, and he will be my son. When he does wrong, I will punish him with a rod wielded by men, with floggings inflicted by human hands. But my love will never be taken away from him, as I took it away from Saul, whom I removed from before you. Your house and your kingdom will endure forever before me; your throne will be established forever.'" Nathan reported to David all the words of this entire revelation. The Lord sent Nathan to David. When he came to him, he said, "There were two men in a certain town, one rich and the other poor. The rich man had a very large number of sheep and cattle, but the poor man had nothing except one little ewe lamb he had bought. He raised it, and it grew up with him and his children. It shared his food, drank from his cup and even slept in his arms. It was like a daughter to him.

"Now a traveler came to the rich man, but the rich man refrained from taking one of his own sheep or cattle to prepare a meal for the traveler who had come to him. Instead, he took the ewe lamb that belonged to the poor man and prepared it for the one who had come to him." David burned with anger against the man and said to Nathan, "As surely as the LORD lives, the man who did this must die! He must pay for that lamb four times over, because he did such a thing and had no pity." Then Nathan said to David, "You are the man! This is what the LORD, the God of Israel, says: 'I anointed you king over Israel, and I delivered you from the hand of Saul. I gave your master's house to you, and your master's wives into your arms. I gave you all Israel and Judah. And if all this had been too little, I would have given you even more. Why did you despise the word of the LORD by doing what is evil in his eyes? You struck down Uriah the Hittite with the sword and took his wife to be your own. You killed him with the sword of the Ammonites. Now, therefore, the sword will never depart from your house, because you despised me and took the wife of Uriah the Hittite to be your own.' "This is what the LORD says: 'Out of your own household I am going to bring calamity on you. Before your very eyes I will take your wives and give them to one who is close to you, and he will sleep with your wives in broad daylight. You did it in secret, but I will do this thing in broad daylight before all Israel.' " Then David said to Nathan, "I have sinned against the LORD."

Nathan replied, "The LORD has taken away your sin. You are not going to die. But because by doing this you have shown utter contempt for the LORD, the son born to you will die." After Nathan had gone home, the LORD struck the child that Uriah's wife had borne to David, and he became ill. David pleaded with God for the child. He fasted and spent the nights lying in sackcloth on the ground. The elders of his household stood beside him to get him up from the ground, but he refused, and he would not eat any food with them. On the seventh day the child died. David's attendants were afraid to tell him that the child was dead, for they thought, "while the child was still living, he wouldn't listen to us when we spoke to him. How can we now tell him the child is dead? He may do something desperate." David noticed that his attendants were whispering among themselves, and he realized the child was dead. "Is the child dead?" he asked.

"Yes," they replied, "he is dead." Then David got up from the ground. After he had washed, put on lotions and changed his clothes, he went into the house of the LORD and worshiped. Then he went to his own house, and at his request they served him food, and he ate.

His attendants asked him, "Why are you acting this way? While the child was alive, you fasted and wept, but now that the child is dead, you get up and eat!"

He answered, "While the child was still alive, I fasted and wept. I thought, 'Who knows? The LORD may be gracious to me and let the child live.' But now that he is dead, why should I go on fasting? Can I bring him back again? I will go to him, but he will not return to me."

Then David comforted his wife Bathsheba, and he went to her and made love to her. She gave birth to a son, and they named him Solomon. The LORD loved him; and because the LORD loved him, he sent word through Nathan the prophet to name him Jedidiah.

Meanwhile Joab fought against Rabbah of the Ammonites and captured the royal citadel. Joab then sent messengers to David, saying, "I have fought against Rabbah and taken its water supply. Now muster the rest of the troops and besiege the city and capture it. Otherwise I will take the city, and it will be named after me."

So David mustered the entire army and went to Rabbah, and attacked and captured it. David took the crown from their king's head, and it was placed on his own head. It weighed a talent of gold, and it was set with precious stones. David took a great quantity of plunder from the city and brought out the people who were there, consigning them to labor with saws and with iron picks and axes, and he made them work at brickmaking. David did this to all the Ammonite towns. Then he and his entire army returned to Jerusalem. **2 Samuel 13** In the course of time,

Amnon son of David fell in love with Tamar, the beautiful sister of Absalom son of David. Amnon became so obsessed with his sister Tamar that he made himself ill. She was a virgin, and it seemed impossible for him to do anything to her. Now Amnon had an adviser named Jonadab son of Shimeah, David's brother. Jonadab was a very shrewd man. He asked Amnon, "Why do you, the king's son, look so haggard morning after morning? Won't you tell me?" Amnon said to him, "I'm in love with Tamar, my brother Absalom's sister." "Go to bed and pretend to be ill," Jonadab said. "When your father comes to see you, say to him, 'I would like my sister Tamar to come and give me something to eat. Let her prepare the food in my sight so I may watch her and then eat it from her hand.'" So Amnon lay down and pretended to be ill. When the king came to see him, Amnon said to him, "I would like my sister Tamar to come and make some special bread in my sight, so I may eat from her hand."

David sent word to Tamar at the palace: "Go to the house of your brother Amnon and prepare some food for him." So Tamar went to the house of her brother Amnon, who was lying down. She took some dough, kneaded it, made the bread in his sight and baked it. Then she took the pan and served him the bread, but he refused to eat.

"Send everyone out of here," Amnon said. So everyone left him. Then Amnon said to Tamar, "Bring the food here into my bedroom so I may eat from your hand." And Tamar took the bread she had prepared and brought it to her brother Amnon in his bedroom. But when she took it to him to eat, he grabbed her and said, "Come to bed with me, my sister." "No, my brother!" she said to him. "Don't force me! Such a thing should not be done in Israel! Don't do this wicked thing. What about me? Where could I get rid of my disgrace? And what about you? You would be like one of the wicked fools in Israel. Please speak to the king; he will not keep me from being married to you." But he refused to listen to her, and since he was stronger than she, he raped her.

Then Amnon hated her with intense hatred. In fact, he hated her more than he had loved her. Amnon said to her, "Get up and get out!" "No!" she said to him. "Sending me away would be a greater wrong than what you have already done to me."

But he refused to listen to her. He called his personal servant and said, "Get this woman out of my sight and bolt the door after her." So his servant put her out and bolted the door after her. She was wearing an ornate robe, for this was the kind of garment the virgin daughters of the king wore. Tamar put ashes on her head and tore the ornate robe she was wearing. She put her hands on her head and went away, weeping aloud as she went. Her brother Absalom said to her, "Has that Amnon, your brother, been with you? Be quiet for now, my sister; he is your brother. Don't take this thing to heart." And Tamar lived in her brother Absalom's house, a desolate woman. When King David heard all this, he was furious. And Absalom never said a word to Amnon, either good or bad; he hated Amnon because he had disgraced his sister Tamar.

Absalom Kills Amnon

Two years later, when Absalom's sheepshearers were at Baal Hazor near the border of Ephraim, he invited all the king's sons to come there. Absalom went to the king and said, "Your servant has had shearers come. Will the king and his attendants please join me?"

"No, my son," the king replied. "All of us should not go; we would only be a burden to you." Although Absalom urged him, he still refused to go but gave him his blessing.

Then Absalom said, "If not, please let my brother Amnon come with us."

The king asked him, "Why should he go with you?" But Absalom urged him, so he sent with him Amnon and the rest of the king's sons. Absalom ordered his men, "Listen! When Amnon is in high spirits from drinking wine and I say to you, 'Strike Amnon down,' then kill him. Don't be afraid. Haven't I given you this order? Be strong and brave." So Absalom's men did to Amnon what Absalom had ordered. Then all the king's sons got up, mounted their mules and fled.

While they were on their way, the report came to David: "Absalom has struck down all the king's sons; not one of them is left." The king stood up, tore his clothes and lay down on the ground; and all his attendants stood by with their clothes torn. But Jonadab son of Shimeah, David's brother, said, "My LORD should not think that they killed all the princes; only Amnon is dead. This has been Absalom's express intention ever since the day Amnon raped his sister Tamar. My LORD the king should not be concerned about the report that all the king's sons are dead. Only Amnon is dead." Meanwhile, Absalom had fled.

Now the man standing watch looked up and saw many people on the road west of him, coming down the side of the hill. The watchman went and told the king, "I see men in the direction of Horonaim, on the side of the hill." Jonadab said to the king, "See, the king's sons have come; it has happened just as your servant said." As he finished speaking, the king's sons came in, wailing loudly. The king, too, and all his attendants wept very bitterly. Absalom fled and went to Talmai son of Ammihud, the king of Geshur. But King David mourned many days for his son. After Absalom fled and went to Geshur, he stayed there three years. And King David longed to go to Absalom, for he was consoled concerning Amnon's death.

- Men will learn the role of the mentor is not always pleasant.
- Men will learn that the mentoring relationship is based upon honesty.
- Men will learn that the mentoring relationship is based upon integrity.
- Men will learn that the mentoring relationship requires courage.
- Men will learn that there are dire consequences for sin.

The leader will assign the men to groups of four or six for discussion about the mentoring event in the scripture. They are to discuss the process of mentoring between Nathan and David.

A recorder is assigned to take notes about the discussion which are to be given to the reporter once completed.

The leader will reassemble the men and use the group to discuss the mentoring incidents according the scriptural text assigned.

Each group reporter will share the highlights of the small group discussion with the larger group.

The leader will lead the large group discussion after the reports have been shared to determine if the men have understood the objectives.

1. **What was Nathan's role in this mentoring story?**
2. **Was Nathan afraid to obey God and confront the king?**
3. **What was David's reaction to Nathan's accusation?**
4. **What were the consequences to David's sin?**
5. **Does mentoring require you to hold the mentoree accountable?**

Reading Assignment:

Proverb each day of the week (group discussion)
Five Psalms each day of the week (daily devotion)

Matthew 4

From *Age-ing* to *Sage-ing* by Zalman Schachter-Shalomi (continue reading)

Objective:

Proverbs gives us wisdom about our horizontal relationship with each other.
Psalms gives us wisdom about our vertical relationship with God.

Session Three

Mentoring in the New Testament

Lesson one (week one)

Jesus initiated mentoring in the New Testament when He saw Peter and gave him the call. Matthew 4:18-22 As Jesus was walking beside the Sea of Galilee, he saw two brothers. Simon called Peter and his brother Andrew. They were casting a net into the lake, for they were fishermen. "Come, follow me", Jesus said, "and I will make you fishers of men." At once they left their nets and followed him. Going on from there, he saw two other brothers, James son of Zebedee and his brother John. They were in a boat with their father Zebedee, preparing their nets. Jesus called them, and immediately they left the boat and their father and followed him.

Procedure:

Every lesson should be preceded with prayer and refreshments. The men are encouraged to share concerns and celebrations at each meeting.

After the group has shared concerns and celebrations, the leader should introduce the next lesson.

Lesson Ice Breaker:

Ask the men to read a few verses from Proverbs according to the date for a discussion as they eat their refreshments.

The leader will discuss how Jesus called the disciples to a mentoring ministry.

They were called to make a total commitment.

Goals & Objectives:

- Men will learn that mentoring is a calling.
- Men will learn that mentoring is a commitment.
- Men will learn that mentoring is a process.
- Men will learn that mentoring is relational.
- Men will learn that mentoring is rooted in love.

The leader will assign the men to groups of four or six for discussion about the mentoring event in the scripture. They are to discuss the process of mentoring between Jesus and His disciples. The discussion will be centered around the following Scriptures:

Matthew 4:19-20 (Mentoring as a calling)

"Come, follow me," Jesus said, "and I will make you fishers of men." At once they left their nets and followed him.

Matthew 5:1-2 (Mentoring as a commitment)

Now when he saw the crowds, he went up on a mountainside and sat down. His disciples came to him, and he began to teach them, saying:

Matthew 5:43-48 (Mentoring as a process)

"You have heard that it was said, 'Love your neighbor and hate your enemy.' But I tell you: Love your enemies and pray for those who persecute you, that you may be sons of your Father in heaven." "He causes his sun to rise on the evil and the good, and sends rain on the righteous and the unrighteous. If you love those who love you, what reward will you get? Are not even the tax collectors doing that? And if you greet only your brothers, what are you doing more than others? Do not even pagans do that? Be perfect, therefore, as your heavenly Father is perfect."

John 13:35 (Mentoring is rooted in love)

By this all men will know that you are my disciples, if you love one another.

A recorder is assigned to make note about the discussion which are to be given to the reporter once completed.

Each group reporter will share the highlights of the small group discussion with the larger group.

The leader should review these scriptures and discuss the meaning and context for clarity and understanding with the men.

Reading Assignment:

Proverb each day of the week (group discussion)
Five Psalms each day of the week (daily devotion)
From Age-ing to Sage-ing by Zalman Schachter-Shalomi (continue reading)

Objective:

Proverbs gives us wisdom about our horizontal relationship with each other.
Psalms gives us wisdom about our vertical relationship with God.

Lesson two (week two)

Mentoring in the New Testament

Barnabas mentored to Paul

Procedure:

Every lesson should be preceded with prayer and refreshments. The men are encouraged to share concerns and celebrations at each meeting.

After the group has shared concerns and celebrations, the leader should introduce the next lesson.

Lesson Ice Breaker:

Ask the men to read a few verses from Proverbs according to the date for a discussion as they eat their refreshments.

Ask one of the men to read the Scripture below about Barnabas and Paul. Encourage the men to discuss the role Barnabas played by supporting Paul and his ministry among the fearful Jews. Lead the men in a discussion about the importance of supporting a mentoree when it is unpopular or even when it is sacrificial.

The leader will assign the men to groups of four or six for discussion about the mentoring event in the scripture. They are to discuss the process of mentoring between Barnabas and Paul.

A recorder is assigned to make note about the discussion which are to be given to the reporter once completed.

Acts 9:26 (NIV)

When he came to Jerusalem, he tried to join the disciples, but they were all afraid of him, not believing that he really was a disciple. But Barnabas took him and brought him to the apostles. He told them how Saul on his journey had seen the Lord and that the Lord had spoken to him, and how in Damascus he had preached fearlessly in the name of Jesus. So Saul stayed with them and moved about freely in Jerusalem, speaking boldly in the name of the Lord.

Objectives:

- Men will learn how Barnabas mentored Paul
- Men will learn how important a mentor can be during a crisis.
- Men will learn the value of a mentoring relationship.

The leader will assign the men to groups of four or six for discussion about the mentoring event in the scripture. They are to discuss the process of mentoring between Nathan and David.

A recorder is assigned to make note about the discussion which are to be given to the reporter once completed. The leader will reassemble the men and use the group to discuss the mentoring incidents according the scriptural text assigned.

Each group reporter will share the highlights of the small group discussion with the larger group. The leader will lead the large group discussion after the reports have been shared to determine if the men have understood the objectives. The leader can determine competency of the lesson taught by asking related questions about the objectives.

1. **What was Paul's situation with the Jews in Jerusalem?**
2. **What was Barnabas' role in helping Paul?**
3. **Why is Barnabas, considered a mentor to Paul?**
4. **How critical was this mentoring relationship for Paul?**

Reading Assignment:

Proverb each day of the week (group discussion)
Five Psalms each day of the week (daily devotion)

Acts 9:26-28

From Age-ing to Sage-big by Zalman Schachter-Shalomi
(continue reading)

Objective:

Proverbs gives us wisdom about our horizontal relationship
with each other.

Psalms gives us wisdom about our vertical relationship
with God.

Lesson three (week three)

Mentoring in the New Testament

Barnabas mentors to John Mark

Procedure:

Every lesson should be preceded with prayer and refreshments. The men are encouraged to share concerns and celebrations at each meeting.

After the group has shared concerns and celebrations, the leader should introduce the next lesson.

Lesson Objective:

* Men will learn how Barnabas mentored John Mark

Lesson Ice Breaker:

Ask the men to read a few verses from Proverbs according to the date for a discussion as they eat their refreshments.

Ask one of the men to read the Scripture below as they assemble into their groups of four or six men. Encourage the men to talk about Barnabas courage to disagree with Paul and to support John Mark by choosing to go with John Mark rather than Paul. Ask the men if they have made unpopular decisions to support someone. Use this opportunity as leader of the group to talk about friends agreeing to be able to disagree and remain friends.

The leader will assign the men to groups of four or six for discussion about the mentoring event in the scripture. They are to discuss the process of mentoring between Barnabas and John Mark.

A recorder is assigned to make note about the discussion which are to be given to the reporter once completed.

Acts 15:36 (NIV)

Sometime later Paul said to Barnabas, let us go back and visit the brothers in all the towns where we preached the word of the Lord and see how they are doing. Barnabas wanted to take John, also called Mark, with them, but Paul did not think it wise to take him, because he had deserted them in Pamphylia and had not continued with them in the work. They had such a sharp disagreement that they parted company Barnabas took Mark and sailed from Cyprus.

Reassemble

The leader will reassemble the men and use the group to discuss the mentoring incidents according the scriptural text assigned.

Each group reporter will share the highlights of the small group discussion with the larger group.

The leader will lead the large group discussion after the reports have been shared to determine if the men have understood the objectives.

The leader can determine competency of the lesson taught by asking related questions about the objectives.

1. **Why was it necessary for Barnabas to mentor John Mark?**
2. **Does Paul's rejection of John Mark cause a problem with Barnabas?**
3. **How does disagreement impact the mentoring relationship?**

Reading Assignment:

Proverb each day of the week (group discussion)
Five Psalms each day of the week (daily devotion)
Acts 15:36-16:5

From Age-ing to Sage-ing by Zalman Schachter–Shalomi
(continue reading)

Note:

Proverbs gives us wisdom about our horizontal relationship with each other.

Psalms gives us wisdom about our vertical relationship with God.

Close the session with a prayer in a circle with men holding hands (encourage intimacy).

Lesson four (week four)

Paul mentored Timothy

Lesson Objectives:

- Men will learn how Paul mentored Timothy
- Men will learn how mentoring impacted the gospel.

The leader could discuss the relationship between Paul and Timothy that is similar to a father and a son. The mentor and mentoree are to develop a close intimate relationship that develops because of the love they have for one another.

The leader will assign the men to groups of four or six for discussion about the mentoring event in the scripture. They are to discuss the process of mentoring between Paul and Timothy.

A recorder is assigned to make note about the discussion which are to be given to the reporter once completed.

Acts 16:1-5

He came to Debra and then to Lystra, where a disciple named Timothy lived, whose mother was a Jewess and a believer, but whose father was a Greek. The brothers at Lystra and Iconium spoke well of him. Paul wanted to take him along on the journey, so he circumcised him because of the Jews who lived in that area, for they all knew that his father was a Greek. As they traveled from town to town, they delivered the decisions reached by the apostles and elders in Jerusalem for the people to obey. So the churches were strengthened in the faith and grew daily in numbers.

Philippians 2:20-23 (NIV)

I have no one else like him, who takes a genuine interest in your welfare. For everyone looks out for his own interests, not those of Jesus Christ. But you know that Timothy has proved himself, because as a son with his father he has served with me in the work of the gospel. I hope, therefore, to send him as soon as I see how things go with me.

Reassemble:

The leader will reassemble the men and use the group to discuss the mentoring incidents according the scriptural text assigned.

Each group reporter will share the highlights of the small group discussion with the larger group.

The leader will lead the large group discussion after the reports have been shared to determine if the men have understood the objectives.

The leader can determine competency of the lesson taught by asking related questions about the objectives.

- Ask the men to reflect on the lesson and to think about the above mentoring pair in the lesson, and which one they identify with. Why?
- What is the exceptional quality about Timothy that impresses Paul?
- What kind of relationship compares to that of Timothy and Paul?

Reading Assignment:

Proverb each day of the week (group discussion)
Five Psalms each day of the week (daily devotion)
Acts
From Age-big to Sage-ing by Zalman Schachter–Shalomi (continue reading)

Note:

Proverbs gives us wisdom about our horizontal relationship with each other.

Psalms gives us wisdom about our vertical relationship with God.

Close the session with a prayer in a circle with men holding hands (encourage intimacy).

Lesson five (week five)

Mentoring in the Early Church

And the things that thou hast heard of me among many witnesses, the same commit thou to faithful men, who shall be able to teach others also. (2 Tim 2:2)

Goals & Objectives:

- Men will learn about the beginning of mentoring in the early Church.
- Men will learn about the selection of mentors and mentorees in the each church.
- Men will learn about the characteristics of mentors in the early church.

Procedure:

Every lesson should be preceded with prayer and refreshments. The men are encouraged to share concerns and celebrations at each meeting.

After the group has shared concerns and celebrations, the leader should introduce the next lesson.

Lesson Ice Breaker:

Ask the men to talk about their earliest experience with a spiritual mentor in their congregation or spiritual life. Allow a few minutes of sharing and begin the lesson.

The leader will assign the men to groups of four or six for discussion about the mentoring event in the scripture. They are to discuss the process of mentoring between Paul and Timothy.

A recorder is assigned to make note about the discussion which are to be given to the reporter once completed.

Mentoring began in the each church with Jesus Christ. Matthew 4:18 (NIV)

As Jesus was walking beside the Sea of Galilee, he saw two brothers. Simon called Peter and his brother Andrew. They were casting a net into the lake, for they were fishermen. "Come, follow me," Jesus said, "and I will make you fishers of men." At once they left their nets and followed him.

Jesus called men to become his disciples. He was asking them to make a complete and total commitment to his mentoring process that was a lifetime commitment. Jesus modeled for us a mentoring model that was intentional, committed, and lifelong.

Mentoring was modeled by Jesus to His disciples

Jesus disciples followed his model of mentoring by seeking others to mentor.

Matthew 10:5-10

These twelve, Jesus sent out with the following instructions: "Do not go among the Gentiles or enter any town of the Samaritans. Go rather to the lost sheep of Israel.

As you go, preach this message: 'The kingdom of heaven is near.' Heal the sick, raise the dead, cleanse those who have leprosy, drive out demons. Freely you have received, freely give. Do not take along any gold or silver or copper in your belts:

Mentoring was practice by the disciples to each other Luke 10:1-3

After this the LORD appointed seventy-two others and sent them two by two ahead of him to every town and place where he was about to go. He told them, "The harvest is plentiful, but the workers are few. Ask the Lord of the harvest, therefore, to send out workers into his harvest field. Go! I am sending you out like lambs among wolves."

The leader can determine competency of the lesson taught by asking related questions about the objectives.

Reading Assignment:

Proverb each day of the week

Five Psalms each day of the week

Acts

From Age-ing to Sage-ing by Zalman Schachter–Shalomi (continue reading)

Note:

Proverbs gives us wisdom about our horizontal relationship with each other.

Psalms gives us wisdom about our vertical relationship with God.

Close the session with a prayer in a circle with men holding hands (encourage intimacy).

Session Four

<u>Mentoring in Culture</u>

Lesson one (week one)

For if you were to have countless tutors in Christ, yet {you would} not {have} many fathers; for in Christ Jesus I became your father through the gospel. (Cor. 4: 15)

Mentoring – The word mentoring in our culture comes from the name of a character in Greek Mythology. Ulysses, the father of Telemachus, hired Mentor to tutor, guide, and educate his son in his absence. The term has been used in this capacity ever since. It is used in academia to describe a relationship between a professor and the student. In corporate America, it describes the relationship between a senior and junior executive, journeymen and an apprentice, and an experience worker and a beginner. In each of these relationships, the mentor is the knowledgeable and skilled person who guides or coaches the unskilled person or the one without knowledge.

- Men will learn to identify *Interactive mentoring*
- Men will learn to identify the level of mentoring called *Occasional Mentoring*
- Men will learn to identify the level of mentoring called *Passive Mentoring*
- Men will learn to identify an *Unintentional mentor*
- Men will learn to identify a *Negative mentor*

Procedure:

Every lesson should he preceded with prayer and refreshments. The men are encouraged to share concerns and celebrations at each meeting.

After the group has shared concerns and celebrations, the leader should introduce the next lesson.

Lesson Ice Breaker:

Ask the men to talk about their earliest experience with a mentor in their culture, community or home. Allow a few minutes of sharing and begin the lesson.

The leader will assign the men to groups of four or six for discussion about the mentoring in the culture. They are to discuss their experiences with mentoring in the work place, school, or other places. They should have someone to read the comments and quotes below and discuss the implications.

A recorder is assigned to make note about the discussion which are to be given to the reporter once completed.

Mentoring in the culture began in early Greek history. The actual term *mentor* is the name of a character in Greek Mythology. He was hired by Ulysses to teach, coach and nurture his son Telemachus. Mentor had a long term relationship with Ulysses' son, Telemachus that had a life time impact.

There were many stories of men having mentors during the research of this project. Many men were mentored by their grandfathers, uncles, and older siblings. Other men were mentored by men in the community,

Zalman Schachter-Shalomi the author of *From Age-mg to Sage-ing*, gives a very good explanation of mentoring in the culture:

> Mentoring preserves valuable life experience from disappearing with the inevitable decay of the physical body. If you work on a computer for an hour and there's a power outage, that work simply disappears from the computer's memory. Similarly if you don't "save" your life experience through mentoring and

through leaving legacies, the wisdom that you have synthesized through decades of difficult learning will disappear as your physical medium of storage and expression wears out. How sad! That's why an elder's heart leaps up when a younger person says. "Please take me on as your student or apprentice. There's so much I want to learn from you."

What do elders have to teach? Over and beyond an exchange of verbal information and technical skills, they transmit what can't be acquired from books. When the transfer of sheer data just isn't sufficient, they impart the wisdom of a lifetime (including the personal attitudes, moral and ethical – judgments, and aesthetic appreciations that characterized them) through the fire of a unique relationship, the give-and-take of a living dialogue with a younger student or apprentice.

When an elder fertilizes a young person's aspiring, mind with his knowledge and seasoned judgment the student receives a living spark, a transmission that may one day blossom into wisdom.[95]

Mentoring in the culture has been a practice dating back to the earliest periods in secular history. It was customary for the teacher to mentor the student over long periods of time whether in the trade schools, or academia. Socrates was the mentor to Plato. Plato was the mentor to Aristotle. All of these men were philosophers, and Socrates was the father of philosophy. He developed a style of questioning that was termed *Socratic Dialogue*. Socrates would talk to whoever would listen, ask questions, criticized answers, and poked holes in faulty arguments. His style influenced Plato, who influenced Aristotle.

---

[95]   Zalman Schachter-Shalomi, *From Age-ing to Sage-ing* (Warner Brooks: New York, 1995), 190-191.

Mentoring occurs in the world of academia when a professor mentors his/her student through the process of obtaining an advanced degree. The professors and students will spend long hours together over three to four years of study. During this time, the professor often shares more with the student than subject matter. The student can also benefit from the professor's wisdom and years of professional studies.

Mentoring was recently initiated in the Detroit Public Schools. The retired teachers were encouraged to return to the classrooms as coaches/mentors to first years teachers. They could establish their own working hours, and days. The incentive to the retired teachers was a salary without penalty to their pensions. The incentive to the first year teacher is coaching or mentoring without judgment or job evaluation.

Sharon E. Davis recently wrote an article in the Front Page, a local newspaper in Detroit, Michigan in, which she expresses the importance of mentors:

> Mentors can act as role model, career counselor or leadership coach. According to Healthy companies' magazine, a recent survey of 1000 employees identified the characteristics of successful people in their organizations.

The top qualities were:

1. Works long hours
2. Has mentor willing to work beyond limit
3. "Connections" more important than performance
4. Makes good presentations
5. Works hard
6. Doesn't stay in one place
7. Meets commitments
8. Loyal

9. Decisive and strong?[96]

The leader should encourage the men to discuss the list of characteristics mentioned in the article to express their opinions about the merits of those characteristics. They should also comment on the reasons for having a mentor that was included in the article by Ms. Davis:

> Why would we need a mentor? It's because knowing your job is not enough to advance on the job. We also need "insider info" on learning the politics and culture of the corporate environment. Getting this information cannot always be learned from a book; a mentor is one way to learn this.
>
> Today, one definition of mentoring is: a developmental, caring, sharing and helping relationship where one person invests time, know-how and effort in enhancing another person's growth, knowledge and skills. And responds to critical needs in the life of the person in ways that prepare the individual for greater productivity or achievement in the future (American Management Association, mentoring). Mentoring takes time.
>
> Generally, mentoring affects another person as a result of personal one-on-one contact, that's why mentoring is needed more than ever today. A mentor offers knowledge, insight, perspective and wisdom.

According to this article, there are three types of mentoring relationships: situational, informal, and formal. The situational mentor relationship tends to be short and isolated interactions. The relationship has no continuity or long term basis. The informal mentoring style can be short or lifetime. It is typically

---

[96]   Sharon E. Davis, "Mentor; Old dogs teaching young dogs new tricks," Michigan Front Page, 22 September 2000, sec. B p.2.

a professor sharing with a student, or a colleague sharing with a trainee on an informal level. This relationship is based upon personal interactions as oppose to a professional interaction. The last model of mentoring mentioned in the article is formal. It is typically a structure program designed by a corporation. The mentoree is most likely evaluated in some way by the mentor in this setting. This mentoring relationship generally last for a long period of time.

The group should continue to discuss the types of mentor relationships below, and to be able to make the distinctions between them.

An Active Mentor

When the mentor goes on a journey of discovery development and sharing with the mentored, that is active mentoring. The mentor is there for the mentoree to guide, counsel, and encourage. The mentor has a desire to see the mentoree maximize their full potential. A teacher becoming interested in the life of his/her student and begins to support the student financially, emotionally and academically, is an active mentor. A publisher sees the potential in a young writer and begins to tutor and encourage the writer, is an active mentor.

An Occasional Mentor

When a person is mentored in a temporary setting for a short period of time on an occasional basis, it is an example of occasional mentoring. The mentor is not consistent in the time or frequency with which the mentoring occurs. The mentoree has no assigned or expected time to be with the mentor: this is occasional mentoring. The group leader should ask the men to discuss their occasional mentor.

A Passive Mentor

When the mentoring is non-deliberate, and there is no accountability, the mentoring is passive. The mentoree is able to benefit from the mentor's presence only because he happens to be in the mentor's area of influence. The mentor may or may not be aware of the mentoree's presence. The mentor might be intentionally mentoring to someone else, and the mentoree learns by observation.

The group leader should ask the men to talk about an active mentor in their lives.

The leader will reassemble the men and use the group to discuss the mentoring incidents according the scriptural text assigned.

Each group reporter will share the highlights of the small group discussion with the larger group.

The leader will lead the large group discussion after the reports have been shared to determine if the men have understood the objectives.

Leader: Ask the men to describe the following mentoring styles:

Active
Interactive
Formal
Informal
Occasional
Passive
Situational

Close the session with a prayer in a circle with men holding hands (encourage intimacy).

Lesson two (week two)

- Men will learn that they had mentors in their churches and/or homes.
- Men will learn that mentors can be positive and negative leaders.
- Men will learn that effective mentoring requires good communication

Skills

- Men will learn to be open and transparent in their mentoring relationship.
- Men will learn that mentoring is also a spiritual journey.
- Men will learn that they had mentors in their churches and/or homes.

Procedure:

Every lesson should be preceded with prayer and refreshments. The men are encouraged to share concerns and celebrations at each meeting.

After the group has shared concerns and celebrations, the leader should introduce the next lesson.

Lesson Ice Breaker:

Ask the men to talk about their earliest experience with a mentor in their church or home. Allow a few minutes of sharing and begin the lesson.

The leader will assign the men to groups of four or six for discussion about the mentoring event in the culture. They are to discuss their experiences with mentoring in the church.

Luke 10:1-3 (NIV)

After this the Lord appointed seventy-two others and sent them two by two ahead of him to every town and place where he was about to go. He told them, "The harvest is plentiful, but the workers are few. Ask the Lord of the harvest, therefore, to send out workers into his harvest field. Go! I am sending you out like lambs among wolves."

Each group reporter will share the highlights of the small group discussion with the larger group.

The leader will lead the large group discussion after the reports have been shared to determine if the men have understood the objectives. The learning can also he made clear with a few questions such as the following:

1. Did you consider the pastor to be a mentor to you?
2. Were there other leaders in the church who were mentors?
3. Was there someone mentoring negatively in the church?

After the questions have been answered and discussed, the leader should summarize the lesson and ask an elder in the group to offer prayer.

The men should be encouraged to call each other and to keep in touch until the next meeting.

Reading Assignment:

Proverb each day of the week
Five Psalms each day of the week
John C. Maxwell, *Developing the Leader within You*

Lesson three (week three)

- Men will learn that mentors can be positive or negative leaders.

Leadership is defined as the ability to meet followers, or the ability to influence, according to the Maxwell book on leadership.[97]

Every lesson should be preceded with prayer and refreshments. The men are encouraged to share concerns and celebrations at each meeting.

After the group has shared concerns and celebrations, the leader should introduce the next lesson.

The leader will assign the men to groups of four or six for discussion about the mentoring event in the culture. They are to discuss their experiences with having been mentored by both positive and negative mentors. The group will select a recorder to take notes of the discussion, and a reporter who will share the highlights of the discussion with the larger group.

The leader will reassemble the men from small groups to the large group for a report on their discussion. After the reports have been done, the leader will summarize the lesson.

The leader can summarize the lesson by emphasizing that the mentor is leader to the mentoree and has great influence and impact on the life and development of the mentoree. The leader should remind the mentors that they are held accountable for their behavior and influence on the mentoree.

The leader can reinforce the lesson by discussing some essential elements of a good leader/mentor such as:

1. A good coach
2. Foster goodwill

---

[97] John C. Maxwell, *Developing The Leader Within You,* (Nashville: Thomas Nelson Publisher, 1993), 1.

3. Sees the glass half-full
4. Patient and able to endure
5. Is enthusiastic about life
6. Has a positive outlook on life
7. The leader can list some elements of a negative leader/ mentor such as:
   1. Lacks an understanding of people
   2. Is difficult to approach
   3. Does not have an imagination
   4. In denial about own problems
   5. Blames others
   6. Is insecure and untrusting
   7. Cannot work as a team player
   8. Is resistant to change
   9. Would rather run before standing

After the questions has been answered and discussed, the leader should summarize the lesson and ask an elder in the group to offer prayer.

The men should be encouraged to call each other and to keep in touch until the next meeting.

Reading Assignment:

Proverb each day of the week
Five Psalms each day of the week
Zalman Schachter–Shalomi, *From Age-ing to Sage-ing*
John C. Maxwell, *Developing the Leader within You*

Lesson four (week four)

Men will learn that mentors should have good communication skills

Proverbs 1:33 (NIV)

"but whoever listens to me will live in safety and be at ease, without fear of harm."

The leader of the group will assign the men to groups of four or six to discuss the essential elements of good communication. They will talk about the following:

1. Listening
2. Attending
3. Responding
4. Caring

The leader can contribute and reinforce the level of comprehension and reading and sharing the following information. Schachter-Shalomi explains the art and effectiveness of communication through the skill of listening:

For a relationship to bear fruit as Friedman describes; the mentor must not be in a hurry to impress his knowledge on the mentee. If the communication is only one-way, from transmitter to receiver, the mentee probably won't stick around for further sessions. The best mentoring involves giving ear to students or apprentices. Young people frequently want to tune out new ideas, and elders can best serve them by listening attentively and nonjudgmentally, without forming premature conclusions that could short-circuit youthful initiative and enthusiasm. As the elder listens, clarification takes place in the mind of the younger person. Sometimes the elder needn't say a word for learning to occur. The greatest transmission often comes from wordless, attentive listening.[98]

The leader should seek responses to the quote just read, and to encourage a dialogue about attentive listening skills.

After the questions have been answered and discussed, the leader should summarize the lesson and ask an elder in the group to offer prayer.

The men should he encouraged to call each other and to keep in touch until the next meeting.

Reading Assignment:

Proverb each day of the week

Five Psalms each day of the week

Zalman Schachter-Shalomi, *From Age-ing to Sage-ing* John C. Maxwell, *Developing the Leader within You*

---

[98]   Zalman Schachter-Shalomi, *From Age-ing to Sage-ing,* (New York: Warner Brooks, 1997), 193.

Lesson five (week five)

Mentoring and spiritual relationships

Procedure:

Every lesson should he preceded with prayer and refreshments. The men are encouraged to share concerns and celebrations at each meeting.

And for this reason I remind one to kindle afresh the gift of God which is in you through the laying on of hands. (2 Timothy 1:6)

The leader can relate to the mentoree that the context for their mentoring experience has been varied and rich but without their knowledge or awareness.

The kinds of mentoring that have taken place in our culture are as follows:

> In the religious sphere, there is a venerable tradition of mentors passing on the living spark of realization from generation to generation. We find such mentoring between Moses and Joshua in the Old Testament and among Jesus and the apostles in the New Testament. We find a similar pattern of mentoring in the family. From the Neolithic age to the dawn of the modern era, for example, young men would learn from their fathers and grandfathers how to wield and fix plows and when and how to sow seed, while young women would learn from their mothers and grandmothers how to care for children, recognize and gather herbs for healing, and set up households. A natural communal support system wove elder wisdom into the fabric of society.[99]

---

[99] Ibid., 191.

Lesson Ice Breaker:

Ask the men to think about their earliest experience with a mentor in their context, community or home. Allow a few minutes before assigning the men to a group.

The leader will assign the men to groups of four or six for discussion about the mentoring event in the context. The men are to share their thoughts about the mentors in their lives, or the absence of a mentor.

The group leader will instruct the group to select a recorder and a reporter in each group of four to six men. The recorder is responsible for taking notes related to the discussion, and the reporter will use the notes to share with the larger group once the men have reassembled.

The group leader will ask the men to reassemble after a fifteen minute discussion. The group reporter will share the information gathered about the group discussion on mentors in the lives of the men.

The group leader can use this opportunity to ask questions of the group to ascertain whether the objective was learned by the men.

1. Who is considered a mentor?
2. What is the role of a mentor?
3. Is mentoring always positive?

The leader summarizes the lesson, and leads the men in prayer before dismissal.

Reading Assignment:

Proverb each day of the week
Five Psalms each day of the week
From Age-ing to Sage-ing by Zalman Schachter-Shalomi
  (continue reading)

Objective:

Proverbs gives its wisdom about our horizontal relationship with each other.

Psalms gives us wisdom about our vertical relationship.

Session Five

Mentors in Context

Lesson one (week one)

Procedure:

Every lesson should be preceded with prayer and refreshments. The men are encouraged to share concerns and celebrations at each meeting.

After the group has shared concerns and celebrations, the leader should introduce the next lesson (week one).

Lesson Ice Breaker:

Ask the men to think about their earliest experience with a mentor in their congregation.

The specific context for this mentoring training is the Bethany Baptist Church and its African American men. The context of the church includes the community where the populations is, predominant African American. The context for this project is the Bethany Baptist Church of Detroit. Michigan.

It is also a Northwest side community in Detroit that is populated by mostly African Americans. The total membership is 536 of which 203 are males representing 38% and 326 females representing 61%. There are approximately 15 to 20 men that are dependable, active and responsible for leadership training and leadership roles within the Bethany congregation. These would be the targeted men for the mentoring training program.

There are approximately 40 to 50 young males to whom these men could become mentors. Some of these young males are being raised by single mothers as head of household, and in need of a male influence in the lives of their sons. The goal of the mentoring training within the church is to equip and prepare men to mentor each other and the boys in the congregation. After which, the mentors can go into the community and mentor others.

Allow a few minutes before assigning the men to a group.

The leader will assign the men to form groups of four or six for discussion about the mentoring even in the context.

- Men will learn about mentoring from a spiritual perspective in the church

The group leader will instruct the group to select a recorder and a reporter in each group of four to six men. The recorder is responsible for taking notes related to the discussion, and the reporter will use the notes to share with the larger group once the men have reassembled.

Matthew 28:19 (NIV)

Therefore, go and make disciples of nations, baptizing them in the name of the Father and of the Son and of the Holy Spirit.

This command to the disciples of Jesus also speaks to men in the context of Bethany Baptist Church. They are called to a ministry of multiplication through evangelism and outreach. Mentoring can be the process for reaching men within the congregation and also without.

The men should discuss their role in the congregation.

The group leader will ask the men to reassemble after a fifteen minute discussion. The group reporter will share the information gathered by the recorder. The group discussion has focused on mentors in the lives of the men.

Note: The leader should be aware that some men will have painful memories related to those who have mentored negatively, while others will have joyful memories. Give the men time to process their feelings and encourage them to talk about their feelings.

The group leader can use this opportunity to ask questions of the group to ascertain whether the objective was learned by the men.

- Who has the role of mentoring in the home?
- Who has role of mentoring in the community?
- Who has the role of mentoring in the church?

Once the leader has guided the discussion around these questions, the group can be encouraged to prepare for the next lesson.

The leader should summarize the lesson, and lead the men in prayer before dismissal.

Reading Assignment:

Proverb each day of the week (begin at Proverb One on the first day of the month)

Five Psalms each day of the week (begin with Psalm One on the first day of the month)

From Age-ing to Sage-ing by Zalman Schachter-Shalomi (continue reading)

Objective:

Proverbs gives us wisdom about our horizontal relationship with each other.

Psalms gives us wisdom about our vertical relationship.

Lesson two (week two)

Objective:

Men will learn the difference between discipleship and mentoring.

Procedure:

Every lesson should he preceded with prayer and refreshments. The men are encouraged to share concerns and celebrations at each meeting.

After the group has shared concerns and celebrations, the leader should introduce the next lesson (week two).

Lesson Ice Breaker:

Ask the men to think about their experience when they joined the church. What were some of the things said and done to them?

The leader will assign the men to groups of four or six for discussion about the mentoring event in the context. The leader should assign the men to discuss the role of discipleship and mentoring. How are they the same and how are they different?

The group leader will instruct the group to select a recorder and a reporter in each group of four to six men. The recorder is responsible for taking notes related to the discussion, and the reporter will use the notes to share with the larger group once the men have reassembled.

The leader can use an easel to write the distinctions between discipleship and mentoring. The men should be engaged in dialogue about each distinction made so that they can learn the differences.

Discipleship Focus:	Mentoring Focus:
Individual	Relationship between two or more
Task	Process
Leader's Objectives	Mentoree's Objectives
Bible knowledge	Bible Relationships
Short term commitment	Long term commitment
Working Relationship	Rooted in Love
Respect for leader	Mutual respect
Learn from leader	Learn from each other

Reassemble

The group leader will ask the men to reassemble after a fifteen-minute discussion.

The group reporter will share the information gathered by the recorder.

The group leader can use this opportunity to ask questions of the group to ascertain if the objective was learned by the men.

What are some of the differences between discipleship and mentoring?

Describe the difference in the relationship between disciples and mentors.

Explain the differences between the commitments to the relationship in discipleship versus reentering.

Reading Assignment:

Proverb each day of the week
Five Psalms each day of the week
From Age-ing to Sage-ing by Zalman Schachter-Shalomi
(continue reading)

Rationale:

Proverbs gives us wisdom about our horizontal relationship with each other.

Psalms gives us wisdom about our vertical relationship.

Lesson three (week three)

Procedure:

Every lesson should be preceded with prayer and refreshments. The men are encouraged to share concerns and celebrations at each meeting.

After the group has shared concerns and celebrations, the leader should introduce the next lesson (week three).

- Men will learn what it means to become a mentor in the church

Procedure:

Every lesson should be preceded with prayer and refreshments. The men are encouraged to share concerns and celebrations at each meeting.

After the group has shared concerns and celebrations, the leader should introduce the next lesson.

Ice Breaker:

Ask the men to think about their first time in the church and who became a mentor to them.

The leader should ask the men to assemble into groups of four or six men. They should select a recorder to take notes as the men discuss the assignment. A reporter should be selected to share the notes with the larger group of men.

Scripture assignment to discuss:
Matthew 28:19 (NIV)

Therefore, go and make disciples of all nations, baptizing them in the name of the Father and of the Son and of the Holy Spirit.

The leader can determine the level of comprehension of the men regarding making disciples and becoming a mentor from a spiritual perspective.

After the discussion for about 15 minutes, the leader should have the men to reassemble for the large group reporting and discussion.

Each group reporter should share the notes on their group's discussion so that the leader can make comments or bring clarity if it is needed.

The leader should ask someone to read Psalm 1:1-3 to establish a scriptural basis for a mentor to engage the mentoree in training as a new- believer in the church.

Psalm 1(NIV)

Blessed is the man who does not walk in the counsel of the wicked or stand in the way of sinners or sit in the seat of mockers. But his delight is in the law of the LORD, and on his law he meditates day and night. He is like a tree planted by streams of water, which yields its fruit in season and whose leaf does not wither. Whatever he does prospers.

Reading Assignment:

    Proverb each day of the week
    Five Psalms each day of the week
    From Age-ing to Sage-ing by Zalman Schachter-Shalomi
        (continue reading)

The leader should summarize the lesson, and lead the men in prayer before dismissal.

Note:

    Proverbs gives us wisdom about our horizontal relationship
        with each other.
    Psalms gives us wisdom about our vertical relationship.

Lesson four (week four)

Lesson Objective:

- Men will practice the skill of listening as a mentor.

Ice Breaker:

The leader can share that most women listen to each other on the phone attentively without attempting to provide counsel or solutions, while men often try to give advice or fix the problem.

The leader will role play the skill of attentive listening by asking one of the participants to share a concern, event, or celebration with him. Then, the leader should listen attentively and give feedback to the participant and the group to indicate that he was listening attentively.

The leader should ask the men to divide up into groups of four or six men to practice listening attentively

The leader should reassemble the men after 1 minute to discuss their reactions and feelings about the exercise.

The leader should reemphasize the importance of the mentor listening to the mentoree, and the need to refrain from giving advice or offering solutions. The important task is to walk on the journey with the mentoree as the mentoree makes his own discoveries and decisions.

The leader should summarize the lesson, and lead the men in prayer before dismissal.

This scripture should be shared with the men as a motivation to mentor at every opportunity to as many men as possible:

2 Timothy 2:2 (NIV)

And the things you have heard me say in the presence of many witnesses entrust to reliable men who will also be qualified to teach others.

Reading Assignment:

Proverb each day of the week
Five Psalms each day of the week
From Age-ing to Sage-ing by Zalman Schachter-Shalomi
(continue reading)

Lesson five (week five)

Lesson Objective:

Post-test

- The leader will summarize the lessons taught during the training and give opportunity for questions and answers

The leader will give a post-test after the summary to determine the degree of comprehension of the mentors in training. (See Appendix two)

The leader will also give an evaluation form for the participants to complete. (See Appendix three)

Reading Assignment

Five books of Psalms (multiply five times the date in the month)

One Chapter of Proverbs (day of the month)

Appendix One

Answers to questions about mentoring:

1. A mentor is more than someone who transmits information, or teaches skills (secular). A mentor is someone who imparts lessons in the art of living and shares wisdom to the mentoree.

2. Mentoring in the spiritual context is a continuation of the Word of God as a revelation to the people of God (spiritual).

3. Mentoring is important in the work place because it is used to guide or teach the mentoree the required skills for success.

4. Mentoring in the place of worship is used to continue the Word of God and the tradition of the church.

5. God

6. Jesus Christ

7. Role model; self-discipline; self manager; mature; respectful; integrity; honesty; faithful; loyal; counselor; friend; teachable; open; accepting; flexible; spiritual; leader; patient; kind; godly; saved.

Appendix Two

Mentoring Post-test

1. What is the secular meaning of the word mentor?

    _____

    _____

    _____

2. What is the spiritual meaning of the word mentor?

    _____

    _____

    _____

3. Give one reason for the need of a mentor in the work place?

    _____

    _____

    _____

4. Give one reason why mentoring is important in the place of worship?

    _____

    _____

    _____

5. Who is the primary mentor in the Old Testament?

    _____

    _____

    _____

6. Who is the primary mentor in the New Testament?

_____

_____

_____

7. What are some of the characteristics of an effective mentor?

_____

_____

_____

8. Describe how discipleship differs from mentoring.

_____

_____

_____

9. Name one of the most important skills a mentor should exercise with the mentoree?

_____

_____

_____

10. Who is the most important mentor to you?

_____

_____

_____

_____

_____

_____

_____

_____

Appendix Three

Evaluation

On a scale of 0 to 10 with 10 being the highest score, and 0 the lowest, give the following ratings.

A. The mentoring training manual instructions were easily understood

1   2   3   4   5   6   7   8   9   10 (circle your choice)

B. The mentoring training manual was well written

1   2   3   4   5   6   7   8   9   10 (circle your choice)

C. The mentoring training manual was well structured

1   2   3   4   5   6   7   8   9   10 (circle your choice)

D. The mentoring training manual was sufficient for training

1   2   3   4   5   6   7   8   9   10 (circle your choice)

Please add comments, suggestions, or criticisms:

_____

_____

_____

_____

_____

_____

_____

Selected Bibliography

Abatso, George, and Yvonne Abatso. *How to Equip the African American Family*. Chicago: Urban Ministries, 1991.

Bey, Theresa M, and Thomas C. Holmes. *Mentoring: Developing Successful New Teachers*. Reston: Association of Teacher Educators, 1990.

Boyd, Stephen B. *The Men We long to Be*. San Francisco: Harper, 1995.

Cavanagh, John R. *Fundamental Pastoral Counseling*. Milwaukee: The Bruce Publishing Company, 1962.

Cobb, Jr., John B. *Theology and Mentoring*. Philadelphia: Fortress Press, 1977.

Cone, James H, and Wilmore S Gayraud. *Black Theology a Documentary History Volume One*. New York: Orbis Books, 1993.

Crabb, Larry. *Men & Women*. Grand Rapids: Zondervan Publishing, 1993.

Dicks, Russell I. *Principles and Practices of Mentoring*. Englewood Cliffs: Prentice-Hall, 1963.

Fisher, Biddy. *Mentoring*. London: Library Association, 1994.

Gerkin, Charles V. *An Introduction to Mentoring*. Nashville: Abingdon Press, 1997.

Godwin, Andre. *The Pastor Counselor*. New York: Holt, Rinehart and Winston, 1965.

Green, Bernard D. *Couseling and Advice Giving in Mentoring*. Iowa: Wm. C. Brown, 1987.

Hicks, Robert. *The Masculine Journey*. Colorado: Navpress, 1993.

Hiltener, Seward. *Preface of Pastoral Theology*. Nashville: Abington, 1958.

Hull, Bill. *The Disciple Making Pastor*. Old Tappan: Revell, 1988.

Hulme, William E. *The Mentoring of Families*. New York: Abingdon Press, 1962.

June, Lee N, and Matthew Parker. *Men to Men*. Grand Rapids: Zondervan, 1996.

Klaver, Dick Brian. *Men at Peace*. Nashville: Thomas Nelson, 1993.

Kunjufu, Jawanza. *Adam Where Are You? Why Most Black Men Don't Go to Church*. Nashville: Copywritten Material, 1994.

Lee, Courtland C. "Saving the Native Son: Empowering Strategies for Young Black Men." *Eric Document*, 1996: 1-102.

Macon, Larry L. *Discipling The African American Men*. Winston-Derek Publishing, 1997.

Maxwell, John C. *Developing The Leader Within You*. Nashville: Thomas Nelson, 1993.

Mays, Benjamin E. *Born to Rebel*. Athens: The University of Georgia Press, 1971.

McIntyre, Donald, Margaret Wilkin, and Hazel Hagger. *Mentoring: Perspectives on School-Based Teacher Education*. Philadelphia: Kogan page, 1993.

Mincy, Ronald B. *Nurturing Young Black Men*. Lanham: National Book, 1994.

Mink, Oscar G, Keith Q Owen, and Barbara P Mink. *Developing High-Performance People The Art of Coaching*. Reading: Addison-Wesley, 1993.

Mullen, Carol A. *Breaking the Circle of One*. New York: Lang, 1997.

Murray, Margo, and Marna A Owen. *Beyond The Myths and Magic of Mentoring*. San Francisco: Jossey-Bass, 1991.

Nance, Terry. *God's Armor Bearer, Book II*. Tulsa: Harrison House, 1972.

Nix, Sheldon D. *Becoming Effective Fathers and Mentors*. Colorado: Cook, 1996.

Oglesby, Jr., William B. *Biblical Themes for Mentoring*. Nashville: Abingdon, 1980.

Oliver, Gary J. *Real Men Have Feelings Too*. Chicago: Moody Press, 1993.

Otes, Wayne E. *Protestant Pastoral Counseling*. Philadelphia: The Westminister Press, 1962.

Parker, Matthew. *The African American Church: How to Start A Men's Health Project*. Detroit: Family Resources, 1997.

Sample, Tex. *Ministry in an Oral Culture-Living Will Rogers, Uncle Remus and Minnie Pearl*. Louisville: Westminister/John Knox Press, 1994.

Schachter-Shalomi, Zalman. *From Ageing to Sageing*. New York: Warner Books, 1995.

Schlessinger, Laura. *Ten Stupid Things Men do to Mess up Their Lives*. New York: Cliff Street Books, 1997.

Timothy, Operation. "Christian Business Men's Committe." Chattanooga, 1955.

Torrey, R. A. *how to bring men to CHRIST*. Springdale: Whitaker House, 1984.

Vanderpool, James A. *Person To Person*. Garden City: Doubleday, 1997.

Vann, Robert. *Principles for Effective Mentoring to Ex-Prisioners*. Washington: Prison Fellowship, 2000.

Walker, Clarence. *Biblical Counseling with African Americans*. Grand Rapids: Zondervan, 1992.

Wilmore, Gayraud. *Black Men in Prison*. Atlanta: ITC Press, 1990.

Yeomans, Robin, John Sampson, and ed. *Mentorship in the Primary School*. Washington: The Falmer Press, 1994.

CHAPTER 6

Summary and Reflections

This project was created in response to a dilemma observed by the writer who was a denominational official of the American Baptist Churches and a member of Bethany Baptist Church. This dilemma is one of social, biblical, theological, and historical significance. The dilemma refers to the significant disproportion of African American males not in attendance of church compared to women and children.

The writer, from observations and discussions with urban African American pastors, has concluded that the increase in active participation and attendance of African American men will also lead to advancing social opportunities. Such opportunities include the strengthening of the African American church, strengthening of African American families and the renewal of inner city communities. The increase in attendance and participation, on the part of African American males, also leads to positive economic and political implications. Men with histories of incarceration and prison records are more likely to have less education, lower paying jobs, and fewer economic opportunities. Consequently, their families are more likely to live in poverty.

The political implications for those with prison records or convictions with felonies have to do with voting rights. One loses the right to vote once incarcerated. The loss of voting power renders one dependent on others for justice and social equity. Many African American men have been negatively impacted by the penal institutions and are in need of positive support from others once released.

An African American man released from prison had the following advice for other prisoners released back into society:

Seek a mentor or someone who is able to disciple you. Seek out a career mentor or a mentor in general-preferably in a local church or possibly through the prison ministry that is available in the institution that you are about to be released from. I have learned that true discipleship and networking are often the most valuable tools that we as African American males can utilize.[100]

The church has a historical role in the development of men in the past, and it must re-visit that role for the future of men in the present. Others have done studies related to this topic and have come to similar conclusions. The church can play a pivotal role in reversing past injustices and inequities in our culture. The church is equipped and empowered to be a change agent in the lives of all people, and particularly in the life of men who have been incarcerated:

For older men, it's late in the game and their habits are set. The best way to reach African American male adults is by one-on-one interaction. Men will not always respond to even the most fervent appeals from the pulpit. Men who are connected to Jesus Christ and to a local church family must make the effort to evangelize other men on their jobs and in their neighborhoods. The best way for them to do that is through "relationship evangelism." As men, we have to make the effort to form friendship and relationships that go past the superficial level and put us in a position to be open with other men about our challenges and struggles, and to show and demonstrate how we have overcome them through our spiritual relationship

---

[100] Lee N. June and Matthew Parker, eds., *Men to Men* (Grand Rapids: Zondervan Publishing House, 1996), 220.

and by following the wisdom outlined in the Word
of God.[101]

The church has a unique opportunity to reach out to men coming
from the above conditions of adversity. The results of the church's
involvement may take the form of increased church attendance or
active participation by men in its congregational life.

Historically, the church has been a place of worship by men
and women equally. Presently, it has become a place mainly
attended by a majority of women and children. African American
men are conspicuously low in attendance in the church. The need
for more men to become active participants in the church is critical
and essential to the health and success of its ministry. The African
American church cannot carry out its mission effectively without
the attendance and participation of African American men.

The biblical and theological basis for using mentoring as
a method by which men can mentor other men is supported
with several scriptural passages. Mentoring was practiced in the
Scriptures when Abraham mentored his nephew, Lot (Genesis 11:
12). Mentoring was evident when Moses was exiled to Midian.
His father–in–law, Jethro, mentored him (Exodus 2 and 3).
Moses gave the foundation for training mentors in the book of
Deuteronomy when he taught the Jews to obey God, and teach
the commandments and statues to one another. Those statues and
lessons are found in Deuteronomy 6:1-10:

> These are the commands, decrees and laws the Lord
> your God directed me to teach you to observe in the
> land that you are crossing the Jordan to possess, so that
> you, your children and their children after them may
> fear the Lord your God as long as you live by keeping
> all his decrees and commands that I give you, and so

---

[101] Matthew Parker, *Teaching our Men Reaching our Fathers* (Detroit: Matthew Parker, 2000) 40.

that you may enjoy long life. Hear, O Israel, and be careful to obey so that it may go well with you and that you may increase greatly in a land flowing with milk and honey, just as the Lord, the God of your fathers, promised you.

Hear, O Israel: The Lord our God, the Lord is one. Love the Lord your God with all your heart and with all your soul and with all your strength. These commandments that I give you today are to be upon your hearts. Impress them on your children. Talk about them when you sit at home and when you walk along the road, when you lie down and when you get up. Tie them as symbols on your hands and bind them on your foreheads. Write them on the doorframes of your houses and on your gates.

The biblical mandate was expressed by Jesus Christ in Luke, chapter 4, as his ministerial goal was lifted up first by Isaiah. Jesus makes the announcement that the focus of his ministry will be on the poor, the oppressed, the sick and the captive. The verses found in the gospel of Luke, indicates that the followers of Christ, specifically the church, should actively participate in the delivery of good news to the poor, healing to the brokenhearted, deliverance to the captives, and recovery of sight to the blind. The plight of some men in our culture and in our churches makes it a biblical and moral imperative for the church to actively engage in a search and rescue mission. Once found, the men need to be saved, healed, restored, and redeemed through the process of mentoring.

Several scripture verses teach us to seek men and to hold them accountable as spiritual leaders in their families. The men of God were to be sober-minded, upright, and blameless. The Christian men are to be role models in the community and in their homes.[102] God created man in his own image and likeness,

---

[102] Titus 1:6–2; 2 NIV.

and appointed him over the earth. Man is also called upon to leave his mother and father and be united as one with his wife.[103] God calls men to be prayerful, lifting up holy hands, and to be without anger or disputing.

Paul explains to Timothy the characteristics that are desirable in men called to the ministry, but these characteristics are also required of male leaders in the church. Every male leader should be responsible and faithful.[104] God calls men to love their wives as Jesus loved the church and gave himself for it. As fathers, men are called upon by the Lord not to exasperate his children, but to bring them up in the training and instruction of the Lord.[105]

First, men are called to be accountable to God. Secondly, men are called to be accountable to each other. This mentoring manual for men is a way to fulfill this accountability.

The purpose of the project is to develop a manual based on Christianity that will guide the training of African American men to mentor other men. This manual was developed for leaders in the church specifically so that African American males will be encouraged to trust and depend upon the church, as they once did. A review of the Literature concerning mentoring reveals that African American men must be reached through the church in an intentional and purposeful ministry that is holistic, continuous, and redemptive. William B. Ogleshy Jr., offers a starting point from which we can understand the importance of mentoring from a biblical perspective:

> In the biblical sense, mentoring is that function of the people of God wherein we "bear one another's burdens, and so fulfill the law of Christ" (Gal.6:2) as the means for participating in the process of reconciliation. Pastoral counseling is rightly understood only in the

---

[103] Genesis 2:18-25 NIV.
[104] 1Timothy 2:8-3; 8-13 NIV
[105] Ephesians 4,5 NIV

context of mentoring and then at the more specific nature of pastoral counseling.[106]

Mentoring should he holistic in its approach with an objective of leading men to healthy relationship with God, other men and women.

Charles V. Gerkin establishes a biblical and theological basis for mentoring that begins with the religious roles of God's people in the Old Testament. Gerkin identifies three models of mentoring:

> Our most reliable source regarding the beginnings of mentoring is, of course, the Bible. Turning first to that source, we learn that the care of the community of, people, who worshiped the one God, Yahweh, required the assignment of leadership roles to certain individuals. Our earliest pastoral ancestors are to be found among the leaders of the ancient people of Israel. From very early in recorded biblical history the custom was established of designating three classes of such leaders: the priests, a hereditary class that had particular responsibility for worship and ceremonial life; the prophets, who spoke for Yahweh in relation to moral issues, sometimes rebuking the community and its stated political leaders: and the wise men and women, who offered counsel of all sorts concerning issues of the good life and personal conduct.[107]

Mentoring has in the past and will in the future exist for the express purpose of providing care to the people of God. Gerkin, just as Wimberly, identifies the narrative approach to mentoring as a valid model for ministering to the people of God. In addition

---

[106]   William Oglesby Jr. *Biblical Themes For Mentoring* (Nashville: Abington, 1980), 39–40

[107]   Gerkin, Charles V. *An Introduction to Mentoring,* (Nashville: Abington, 1997), 23.

to a biblical and theological basis for mentoring this project also incorporates a cultural perspective.

The study of the African American male first requires a look at the African American family. Drs. George and Yvonne Abatso have done some comprehensive and extensive studies of the African American Family. They, offer a summary of the plight of African American families in America from slavery to contemporary times. Drs. George and Yvonne Abatso explain how the changes in the movements and migration of African American families from the South to the North, and from extended families to nuclear families have weakened the family and the church.

They suggest that the church has to become equipped anew to deal with the contemporary problems that plaque the African American community. The authors identified the factors that have impacted the African American families:

> Today's Black family finds itself in a dilemma due to both external and internal factors, and the family is in a crisis. Statistics reflect trends in the condition of African American families. From 25 to 30% of all young Black males are either in prison or on probation, but supervised by the courts in some way. That is, at least 114 of Black youths are in jail or under the control of the judicial system. About 75% of African American children are being raised in poverty. Before Black babies are born, during the pre-natal stage and throughout the first two years of life, the level and type of nutrition is directly related to their brain development. Many suffer from poor nutrition, and can be expected to develop related problems. Nutrition will affect their development in infancy and their ability to profit from schooling. Another factor affecting African American families is divorce. One out of three Black marriages ends in divorce. This adds to the number of families in,

which children will be reared by single parents. This also will affect their well-being, seeing that whether Black or white, single parents are at the bottom of the poverty scale.[108]

Again, the absence of African American men in particular, has a very negative impact on the African American family's survival. The focus on African American men through mentoring will strengthen the African American family and church. It is essential for the church to be intentional in reaching African American men if the church and community are going to become what it once was to the African American people. The African American community was positive in the midst of a larger negative society. The African American community could offer support and encouragement to its members when it could not be found anywhere else. The church and community can reclaim its prominence and influence with the rescue of African American men.

The holistic care for African American men through mentoring will address those issues of church membership and attendance relationship building. An approach to developing a holistic mentoring for men in the Bethany Baptist Church and its Westside community is "mentoring." A model of men mentoring men will be developed in a manual (see chapter 7).

The initial step in the project was the observation that male membership and attendance in the Bethany Baptist Church was significantly less than that of women. The first thing that was done was to develop a survey of the men in the church and community. The survey was done to ascertain the reasons men do not attend church. The first survey was done orally and informally. The interviewer was doing a unit of Clinical Pastoral Education, and was at the emergency room for several weekends. Most of the men

---

[108] Abatso, George, and Yvonne Abatso. *How to Equip the African American Family*. Chicago: Urban Ministries, 1991.

surveyed orally, were in the emergency room of a local hospital. Usually it was other African American men that had injured the men in the emergency. When interviewed orally, most of the men exhibited negative impressions of the church and church leaders. They expressed a dislike and distrust of preachers and pastors. The men believed that the women were giving their money to the preachers, and that the preachers were wasting the money, or using it to fulfill personal desires. After having done the oral interview, a written interview was developed and administered in the hospital, church, and the local East side community of the Bethany Baptist Church. The survey format used is located in the appendices.

Interviews of the pastors with successful male ministries revealed that men wanted shared leadership with the pastors, and a significant role in the church. The pastors with successful male ministries also had a specific focus on men in the congregation, and made special efforts to attract the men to the congregation, and they did specific things to maintain the men's attendance and participation. The responses from the interview with pastors and African American men aided the development of this mentoring manual.

The manual was designed to help men develop a relationship with God and with each other. The establishment of a trusting relationship is primary and essential in a mentoring process. The men were encouraged to share each other's life journey as a way of initiating conversation and exchange. The rules were established about confidentiality and trust. The men were allowed to share with each other without concern for being judged or belittled. The goal of the sharing is to establish a bond between the men as they disclose to each other. One of the primary lessons for men to learn in the mentoring process is the sacredness of a relationship, and the commitment one makes to a relationship. Many men have experienced difficulties in establishing healthy relationships with both men and women. Some men have experienced pain and disappointment from those with whom they have developed relationships in the past. Consequently, some men are skeptical or reluctant to establish new relationships.

Procedure

A manual was developed to reflect those comments in the surveys of men in the church and community. Lessons were also developed to reflect the comments and suggestions of pastors surveyed. There were lessons taught from the manual to men in Bethany Baptist Church. There were 15 men agreeing to meet on Saturday mornings for five weekends. The men were taught two lessons each weekend, for a total of ten lessons from the manual. The men were encouraged to attend each meeting on time (8:00am to 10:00am) Breakfast food was served each morning the men met. It proved to be a powerful incentive for the men arriving on time, and also for regular attendance.

Research Design

The research question was: "Will men attendance in church increase and will they become more active participants in church after having been mentored by other men in the church?" The goals were to increase the attendance and active participation in the church by men so that the church could become more effective in its ministry and the men more effective in their families and communities.

The project began with an assessment of the men's attitude toward church and church leadership. Oral interviews were made of men in the church, in the community, and in a local hospital. After the oral interviews, the writer developed written surveys so that the responses of men could be documented. The first survey was developed and rejected because consultants to the project mentioned that some of the questions being asked of the men were inappropriate and intrusive. Another survey (see appendix 1) was developed to be distributed throughout churches in the Detroit community and it was also rejected (see appendix 2).

Finally, the writer developed the survey that was acceptable (see appendix 3) and it was given to African American men in the churches and the surrounding communities. The surveys were given to approximately 150 men, 60% were completed and returned. Approximately 85% of the men surveyed were Baptist and 1% consisted of Apostolic, Presbyterian and other faiths. The respondents were very eager to share their views and opinions about the church and its leadership once they knew how the information would be used.

Fifty questionnaire forms (see appendix 5) along with the manual (see appendix 6) were developed for this project and randomly mailed to pastors and lay-leaders throughout the United States. A self-addressed envelope was sent with the manual so that the surveys could be returned to the researcher once completed. There were a total of 34 completed questionnaires returned. Seventeen responses from pastors were returned, and sixteen from the lay-leaders.

The first goal of the project was to contact pastors to determine if there were successful men's ministries in the churches. A list of names of local and national pastors was secured for the purpose of a survey. The survey was designed to determine if the pastors of these churches had successful men's ministries. The most significant goals of the project were to increase attendance and active participation of men in the church.

The political climate of America in the last two decades suggest, that it is very unlikely that the government will continue to offer funds to address the problems impacting the survival of African American men. Blake and Darling express their opinion of the future for African American men in their Journal of Black Studies:

Socioeconomic and political indicators illustrate that African American males are facing an unprecedented crisis because it is difficult for them to acquire self-confidence and self-esteem within the chaos of modern economic and social life (Marable, 1984). The tools to address the problem have been diminished by the federal government. Funds for employment and training programs as well as income support have been curtailed (Joe, 1987). The African American male has been left to fend for himself.

Although this article does not offer solutions to the dilemmas of the African American male, it identifies areas that have caused their familial and social strife. The perpetuation of negative stereotypes by society, and the hidden history of successful African American males, has handicapped them in their struggle to achieve. The contrasting plethora of history available on slavery disillusions them into a submissive and inferior attitude and deters them from a tradition of triumph and success in the mist of suffering.

The African American male is his own liberator, and regardless of the abundance and loyalty of his allies he either must save himself or be lost forever (Karenga, 1986). The African American male is ready to he accepted as part of the American society and no longer he labeled the American problem.

What steps can be taken to integrate the African American male into American society? First, future research will have to concentrate more on holistically examining the dilemmas of the African American male instead of continuing to do research on isolated problems such as crime, violence, and unemployment.

Secondly, social action will be crucial to improve the image of the African American male. Education is an important step in this direction. Families, governments, educational institutions, and community organizations will have to come together to keep more African American males in school until they graduate and/or acquire the necessary academic skills. The creation of new employment and training programs to increase the labor force participation of the African American male will also help him to fulfill the male role of family provider and thus increase family stability.[109]

In conclusion, the churches must adopt a mentoring model to address the plight of African American men if African American men are going to develop coping skills to survive in the 21st Century. The church alone can offer the programs that will address the situation of the African American male with a comprehensive holistic mentoring program. This mentoring model in the hands of pastors and those trained in mentoring can be a tremendous tool and opportunity to seek, disciple, and mentor the African American men in their churches and communities. This specific model will be used to meet the identified needs of African American men in Bethany Baptist Church of Detroit, and its Westside community.

---

[109]   Ibid., 412–413.

Appendix One

(Survey of Pastors)
Rev. Dr. Jerome P. Stevenson, Sr.

Dayton, Ohio 45417

Phone # 937-361-6201
Email: jsteven681@hotmail.com

Transforming/Hope Ministries
4641 Hoover Avenue
Dayton, Ohio 45417
Phone # 937-268-2663 ~ Fax # 937-268-2219

Dear Pastor,

My name is Dr. Jerome P. Stevenson Sr. I serve as the pastor of the Transforming/Hope Ministries Church, of Dayton. I developed a mentoring manual for African American men and would appreciate you helping me by answering these questions.

Please use the self-addressed envelope and mail the survey hack to me as soon as possible.

Please feel free to attach an additional page if you need more space for your responses

Your name (Optional)

_____

Name of church (Optional)

_____

Year church was founded _____

Location of church   Urban ( )   Suburban ( )   Rural ( )

                               North ( )   South ( )   East ( )

                               West ( )   Mid-West( )

Pastors with successful Male Ministries

Please circle your response to each item or question:

A. Sex
   Male   Female

B. Age
   20-29
   30-39
   40-49
   50-59
   60-69
   70 and up

B. Years in Ministry
   1-5
   6-10
   11-15
   16-20
   21-25
   26-30
   30 and up

C. Size of Congregation
   50-100
   100-399
   400-699
   700-999
   1,000-1,299
   1,300 and up

D. Male Membership
   10-19%
   20-29%
   30-39%
   40-49%
   50 and up

Please circle your response to each item or question:

1. **Pastors are aware that males do not attend church because it is not manly or masculine?**

   a. Strongly Agree   b. Agree   c. Uncertain   d. Disagree   e. Strongly Disagree

2. **Pastors should provide mentoring to hurting males?**

   a. Strongly Agree   b. Agree   c. Uncertain   d. Disagree   e. Strongly Disagree

3. **Pastors should help males practice prayer?**

   a. Strongly Agree   b. Agree   c. Uncertain   d. Disagree   e. Strongly Disagree

4. **Pastors should help males develop some personal relationship with others?**

   a. Strongly Agree   b. Agree   c. Uncertain   d. Disagree   e. Strongly Disagree

5. **Pastors should help males develop a strong relationship with God?**

   a. Strongly Agree   b. Agree   c. Uncertain   d. Disagree   e. Strongly Disagree

6. **Pastors should provide worship that supports male participation in church?**

   a. Strongly Agree   b. Agree   c. Uncertain   d. Disagree   e. Strongly Disagree

7. **Pastors should use contemporary language to minister to young males?**

   a. Strongly Agree   b. Agree   c. Uncertain   d. Disagree   e. Strongly Disagree

8. **Pastors should provide fellowship opportunities for males?**

   a. Strongly Agree   b. Agree   c. Uncertain   d. Disagree   e. Strongly Disagree

9. **Pastors should provide educational ministries for males?**

   a. Strongly Agree   b. Agree   c. Uncertain   d. Disagree   e. Strongly Disagree

10. **Pastors should provide career seminars for males?**

    a. Strongly Agree   b. Agree   c. Uncertain   d. Disagree   e. Strongly Disagree

11. **Pastors should provide evangelistic outreach for males?**

    a. Strongly Agree   b. Agree   c. Uncertain   d. Disagree   e. Strongly Disagree

12. **Pastors should provide marital training seminars for males?**

a. Strongly Agree   b. Agree   c. Uncertain   d. Disagree   e. Strongly Disagree

13. **Pastors should provide fatherhood training for males?**

a. Strongly Agree   b. Agree   c. Uncertain   d. Disagree   e. Strongly Disagree

14. **Pastors should provide support groups for divorced males?**

a. Strongly Agree   b. Agree   c. Uncertain   d. Disagree   e. Strongly Disagree

15. **Pastors should provide a bible study for males only?**

a. Strongly Agree   b. Agree   c. Uncertain   d. Disagree   e. Strongly Disagree

16. **Pastors should provide adult literacy training for males?**

a. Strongly Agree   b. Agree   c. Uncertain   d. Disagree   e. Strongly Disagree

17. **Pastors should help males understand their Christian responsibilities?**

a. Strongly Agree   b. Agree   c. Uncertain   d. Disagree   e. Strongly Disagree

18. **Pastors should address critical social issues impacting men?**

a. Strongly Agree   b. Agree   c. Uncertain   d. Disagree   e. Strongly Disagree

19. **Pastors should emphasize spiritual development in men?**

a. Strongly Agree   b. Agree   c. Uncertain   d. Disagree   e. Strongly Disagree

20. **Pastors should use only men in leadership positions?**

a. Strongly Agree   b. Agree   c. Uncertain   d. Disagree   e. Strongly Disagree

21. **Pastors should address racial issues with men?**

a. Strongly Agree   b. Agree   c. Uncertain   d. Disagree   e. Strongly Disagree

22. **Pastors should address sexism issues with men?**

a. Strongly Agree   b. Agree   c. Uncertain   d. Disagree   e. Strongly Disagree

23. Pastors should offer shared leadership with men in their congregations?

a. Strongly Agree   b. Agree   c. Uncertain   d. Disagree   e. Strongly Disagree

24. Pastors should offer shared leadership with females in the congregations?

a. Strongly Agree   b. Agree   c. Uncertain   d. Disagree   e. Strongly Disagree

25. Pastors should encourage only men to enter the ministry as a profession?

a. Strongly Agree   b. Agree   c. Uncertain   d. Disagree   e. Strongly Disagree

Again, I thank you for taking your valuable time to respond to these questions. Your answers will assist me in the development of this "men mentoring to men" manual, which is so critical and essential.

Please write your responses to the following questions on the next page; your comments are very important to this project.

1. **Identify other issues shared with you that were preventing men from attending church?**

   _____

   _____

2. **How was the church affected by the absence of men and their lack of participation?**

   _____

   _____

3. **How do you get men to attend church on a regular basis?**

   _____

   _____

4. **What are you doing to retain men's participation in the church?**

   _____

   _____

5. **What role can women play in the effort to seek and disciple men in the church?**

   _____

   _____

6. **What else can be used to increase men's membership and participation in the church?**

   _____

   _____

7. **What resources have contributed to your men's ministry?**

_____

_____

8. **What role do the men play in your congregation?**

_____

_____

My first attempt to interview the men for this project was done orally in the emergency room of a local city hospital. I was serving as an on-call chaplain in the emergency room. Many of the emergency cases that occur in the late hours of the night and early hours of the morning are related to violent acts committed between men. Usually, the men are of African American descent. I interviewed them to determine if they were members of any church or if they had ever belonged to a church. Their response was an overwhelming no in most of the interviews. Some of the men expressed negative impression of the preachers and pastors, even when they did have contact or knowledge of the church. There seems to have been a general hostility toward the church and the pastor for those men who had never had continuous involvement with the church. Some expressed admiration for the church and their need to return. I did not use these interviews, because they had not been done scientifically or in a scholarly manner for documentation.

There were other written attempts to survey men in the church and community, but those surveys, I was told, were too intrusive and irrelevant. I adjusted the surveys, and the results are in the appendixes.

Appendix Two

African American Male Survey

This is a brief survey to help me (Ashland Theological Seminary Doctoral Student) develop a ministry model for African American males through mentoring in metropolitan Detroit. Please fill it out as completely as possible. All the information you provide will he considered confidential and individual surveys will not be made public.

Date ___/___/___/___

Background:

1) Residence: ____ House ____ Apartment ____ Shelter ____ Other ____

2) Age:

3) Marital Status: ____ Single ____ Married
   ____ Separated ____ Divorced
   ____ Widowed ____ Live Together

4) Were you raised by your:
   ____ Mother ____ Father ____ Grandparents ____ Other

5) Number of children or dependents:

6) Number who live with you:

7) Education: (check highest level completed)
   ____ High School/GED
   ____ Technical, Vocational or Business
   ____ Some College
   ____ College Graduate
   ____ Graduate School

8) Spirituality or Religious Functioning   (Yes) ____ (No) ____
   Believes in God or a Higher Power   (Yes) ____ (No) ____
   Has a personal relationship with God   (Yes) ____ (No) ____
   Reads the Bible or Spiritual Literature or   (Yes) ____ (No) ____
   Prayer Book

9) Name of your current Religion/Faith **Active** (Yes) ____ (No) ____
   Name and Address of Home Church

_____

Chemical Dependency
Have you ever been in a Twelve-Step Program? (Yes) _____ (No) _____
AA _____ NA _____ Other _____ Sponsor   (Yes) _____ (No) _____
Active in Program   (Yes) _____ (No) _____

10) Do you have a support group?   (Yes) _____ (No) _____
    Family _____ Friends _____ Church _____Other _____ None _____

11) What brings you to the hospital?   Medical
    Diagnosis _____
    Know _____ Don't know _____ Self-admit _____
    Yes _____ No _____ Other _____ Whom? _____

12) Employment Status (check correct category
    Employed _____ Unemployed _____ Retired _____ Student _____ Other ___

13) Check the service that would benefit you the most:
    _____ Religious Counseling
    _____ Family Counseling
    _____ Secular Counseling
    _____ Drug or Alcohol Counseling
    _____ Group Support Counseling
    _____ High Blood Pressure Counseling
    _____ Cancer Counseling
    _____ Diabetes Counseling
    _____ HIV Counseling
    _____ AIDS Counseling

14) Have you ever been incarcerated?
    (Yes) _____ (No) _____ If yes, how many times? _____

15) Did you attend church or Sunday School as a child? (Yes) _____ (No) _____

16) Do you believe in God or a higher power?   (Yes) _____ (No) _____

17) How important is it to believe in God or a higher power?

18) Very important _____ Important _____ Not very important _____
    Not important at all _____

19) How often do you pray?
    Everyday _____ Several times per day _____ Every week _____
    Every month _____ Seldom _____ Never

20) How often do you think about dying?
    All the time _____ Often _____ Seldom _____ Never _____

Appendix Three

African American Male Survey

This is a brief survey to help me (Ashland Theological Seminary Doctoral Student) develop a ministry model for African American males through mentoring in metropolitan Detroit. Please fill it out as completely as possible. All the information you provide will be considered confidential and individual surveys will not he made public.

Date __/___/___   Age ____   Zip Code _____

1. **What is it about the church that has kept men away?**

    _____

    _____

    _____

2. **What programs or activities would men like to see in the church?**

    _____

    _____

    _____

3. **What kind of leader or pastor do men want to see in the church?**

    _____

    _____

    _____

4. Why don't men participate in church activities?

_____

_____

_____

5. How have men been damaged or hurt by the church?

_____

_____

_____

Appendix Four

Some "Shoulds" for Mentoring

Principle #1 Self-reliance

Self-reliance is facilitated when the protégé receives encouragement and unconditional acceptance.

Encouragement comes through knowing what to do, how to do it and having the opportunity to do so. Encouragement also comes through knowing that mistakes and failures are not final or irreversible. Mentoring offers training in requisite skills for success in the defined environment, opportunities to practice those skills in meaningful contexts, and the opportunity to learn from those efforts. An underlying attitude of unconditional acceptance confirms the protégés unchanged acceptability as a person, regardless of the success or failure in the task(s). A mentoring environment must be safe where the protégé can feel free to try new things without fear of non- retrievable losses.

Principle #2 The limits on the comprehensiveness

The limits on the comprehensiveness of the mentoring relationship are defined through mutual consent of the mentor(s) and the protégé.

Mentoring cannot be mandated; mentors must be willing to help and the protégé must be willing to receive their help before mentoring can proceed. Mentor offered his help to Telemachus but it was Telemachus who made the decision to accept or reject *Mentor's* help. Mentoring in beginning teacher induction programs where fellow teachers serve as mentors is often inhibited by reluctance on the part of the mentor and or the protégé to initiate such a relationship. Feared *presumptiveness* on the part of the mentor and reluctance to admit *inadequacy* by the protégé are often cited as barriers to be overcome in establishing mentoring relationships. Mentoring, when viewed as a function, can be provided by many and entered into informally to reduce the negative connotations sometimes associated with superior-subordinate relationships. People are usually more willing to offer and to receive help when such behaviors are accepted norms in the situation.

Principle #3 The comprehensiveness of a mentoring effort

The comprehensiveness of a mentoring effort is a function of the resources and expertise made available to the protégé.

Mentoring is it comprehensive effort towards helping the protégé in the development of self-reliance, and personal accountability. The literature on mentoring and mentoring-protégé relationships suggests that a mentor has exclusive responsibility for training the protégé. This is an ominous responsibility from, which many people, who have a great deal to offer, retreat. The comprehensiveness can be increased by assembling and effectively utilizing a variety of available resources. It is not reasonable to assume that one very competent person can provide as much help and expertise as several equally competent people. The idea of mentoring can be extended by including a variety of people in any effort to assist another, assuming of course that each individual is willing to provide such help. Mentoring may include coordinating the efforts and expertise of others in the helping effort. A mentor teacher may initiate contacts for the beginning teacher with other capable teachers in the same building and in doing so provide the beginning teacher with the opportunity to be in contact with additional expertise.

Principle #4:

The comprehensiveness of a mentoring effort is a function of the generalizability within the defined environment of the attitude, skills and behaviors developed by the protégé.

A mentor-protégé relationship will be more comprehensive if the protégé is helped to develop attitudes, skills and behaviors that have broad application and utility within the defined environment. Any mentor-protégé relationship is limited in what it can accomplish given the limits of time and availability of resources. Mentoring efforts should yield maximum returns on any and all resources invested in hoping the protégé. For instance, it was impossible for *Mentor* to teach Telemachus all the specifics he would need to know to function effectively in life. In fact, if *Mentor* had tried he would have failed because part of what Telemachus needed to learn was how to think, reason, and learn for himself. Mentors who take upon themselves the responsibility of providing answers for their protégés inhibit the ability of their protégés to find out for themselves. The saying, "Give a man a fish and you feed him once but teach him to fish and you feed him for life," is very appropriate when trying to provide comprehensive help toward self-reliance.

Principle #5 Mentors growth of their protégé

Mentors should put the growth of their protégé above their own needs except where both can be served without sacrificing the former.

Some individuals engage in helping efforts out of needs within themselves that run counter to the growth of the person they extend themselves toward. Coppersmith and Feldman (1974) make a very good point that those who offer help need to separate their need to provide help from the other person's need to receive help. Mentoring should never involve doing something for a person that the person can benefit most by doing it for him herself. Mentoring is helping not substituting for the protégé. Efforts towards helping another develop self-reliance should not build dependency.

Principle #6 Self-reliant helping others to become the same

People who are themselves self-reliant are more willing and able to help others become the same.

Those who engage in mentoring efforts are likely to be more effective if they have developed or are working to develop appropriate attitudes and skills within themselves. The theories cited to support the definition of mentoring (*i.e.* attribution theory, etc.) also suggest that self-reliant people are more likely than dependent people to:

- Seek new opportunities with a positive attitude, anticipating success.
- Cooperate with others without competition or need to control.
- Be genuine in all their relationships and allow others to do the same.
- Accept the change and obligation of meeting their needs.
- Make their own decisions and not be unduly influenced by others.
- Be productive and make a positive contribution to the quality of life for themselves and others.

Individuals who wish to help others should begin with some introspection to determine their own motives and progress toward self-reliance. They should become aware of their own attitudes and behavior as they are likely to impact on their ability to help others with proper intent and effective action.

These few principles are a beginning point. They provide some direction for designing and implementing mentoring efforts and allow a great deal of latitude in how they are implemented through the configurations of mentoring efforts.[110]

---

[110] Richard S. Kay *A Definition for Developing Self-Reliance Mentoring: Developing Successful New Teachers* ed. Theresa M. Bey and C. Thomas Holmes (Reston: Association of Teachers Educators 1990), 31-36.

Appendix Five

Please answer these questions by circling the answers on a scale of 1 to 10, with ten being the highest score in value.

1 - Lowest Rating   **10** - Highest Rating

The presentation of the manual is good
1   2   3   4   5   6   7   8   9   10
The content of the manual is well written
1   2   3   4   5   6   7   8   9   10
The instructions in the manual are easy to follow
1   2   3   4   5   6   7   8   9   10
The sequences of the lessons were appropriate
1   2   3   4   5   6   7   8   9   10
The questions asked in the lessons were easily understood
1   2   3   4   5   6   7   8   9   10
The directions to the trainer were easily understood
1   2   3   4   5   6   7   8   9   10
You would use this manual to train the men in your congregation
1   2   3   4   5   6   7   8   9   10
You would recommend this manual to your colleagues in the ministry
1   2   3   4   5   6   7   8   9   10
You would purchase this manual if it was for sale
1   2   3   4   5   6   7   8   9   10
The manual is well constructed
1   2   3   4   5   6   7   8   9   10

Please make any suggestions and comments below.

_____
_____
_____

Appendix Six

DEVELOPING A TRAINING MANUAL FOR
MEN MENTORING MEN AT THE
BETHANY BAPTIST CHURCH
OF DETROIT, MICHIGAN AND ITS
WESTSIDE COMMUNITY

BY JEROME P. STEVENSON, SR.

19952 VAUGHAN STREET
DETROIT, MI 48219

A PROJECT PROPOSAL
PRESENTED TO THE FACULTY OF
ASHLAND THELOGICAL SEMINARY
IN PARTIAL FULFILLMENT OF THE REQUIREMENTS
FOR THE DEGREE OF
DOCTOR OF MINISTRY

MAY, 2002

Purpose:

The purpose of this project is to develop a discipleship manual that focuses on mentoring African American men toward achieving increased participation and attendance in the local church. The research question, poised in this project is: In what ways will equipping African Americans men to mentor men result in increased active participation and attendance at the Bethany Baptist Church?

Overview:

The focus of this project is to develop a manual for discipling men at the Bethany Baptist Church. This project seeks to create a manual that will develop men as mentors in the Bethany Baptist Church. It will be a guide for discipling men to become mentors to other men in order to increase active participation and attendance in the church.

The function of this project is to recruit men at the Bethany Baptist Church to become mentors to other men following a twenty-five week training program. The mentors will be assigned to the men of Bethany Baptist Church and prepared for outreach to other men in its Westside Community.

The focus and function of this project presupposes that men to men mentoring are an effective tool by which there can be an increase in male participation and attendance in the local church.[111] In addition, this project presupposes that men who are active participants in the church will positively impact families and communities.

Rationale:

This project is the outcome of a need observed by the writer who is a denominational official with the American Baptist Churches

---

[111] Proverbs 27:17

and a member of the Bethany Baptist Church on the Westside of Detroit. The writers observations together with concerns expressed by African American pastors serving inner-city churches suggest opportunities if there is an increase in active participation and attendance of African American men in local churches, the increased active participation and attendance of African American men, it is suggested, will contribute to strengthening the church, families and communities. Consistently, across urban communities in the United States, this phenomenon of low numbers of African American men, who actively participate and attend church in relation to that of African American women, is the norm. The need to strengthen churches, families and communities, African American pastors suggest this correlated with increasing participation and attendance of African American men in the ministries of the local church. Also, a consistent observation suggests that a constructive future for this inner city congregation, its families and community are seriously threatened. The consistency of this phenomenon in urban African American churches further suggests a systemic issue that has political and social implications.

There exist biblical foundations for guiding this project. The biblical narrative relating to the destruction of Sodom and Gomorrah reveals the significance God places on the presence of righteous men in the community. God spoke to Abraham and told him He would not destroy the city if he could find fifty righteous men.[112]

The account of Rahab's intervention on behalf of two righteous men served to spare her family's posterity and the blessing of the land.[113] Judah the nation, shared the plight of the absence of men when the scripture records. And I sought for a man among them that should make up the hedge, and stand

---

[112] Genesis 18:26
[113] Joshua 6:17–23

in the gap before me for the land, that I should not destroy it: but I found none.[114] Paul writing to Timothy provides biblical foundation for a discipling model that guides the development of manual that will train men to mentor men that will result in increased participation and attendance of men at the Bethany Baptist Church.[115]

Historical events impacting African American life such as slavery in America and systemic racism and discrimination have hearing on the participation and attendance of African American men in local urban churches. One particular incident worthy of mentioning is a letter written by Willie Lynch that guided the attitudes of American slave owners and, no doubt, a white culture that continues to practice racism and oppression. Willie Lynch, a slave owner in the West Indies in 1717, identities strategies to be used by White stave owners in America for controlling the slaves. He states in the *"Willie Lynch letter: The Making of a Slave:"* [116]

> I have outlined a number of differences among the slaves: and I take these differences and make them bigger. I use fear, distrust, and envy for control purposes. These methods have worked on my modest plantation in the West Indies and it will work throughout the South. Take this simple little list of differences, and think about them. On top of my list is "Age", but is there only because it starts with and "A;" the second is "color" or shade, there is intelligence, size, sex, size of plantations, status on plantation, attitude of owners, whether the slaves live in the valley, on a hill, East, West, North, South, have fine hair, coarse hair, or is tall or short. Now that you have a list of differences, I shall give you an

---

[114] Ezekiel 22:30

[115] 2 Timothy 2:2

[116] http://www.finalcall.com/artman/publish/Perspectives_1/Willie_Lynch_letter_The_Making_of_a_Slave.shtm l

outline of action–but before that I shall assure you that distrust is stronger than trust and envy is stronger than adulation, respect, or admiration.

The Black slave after receiving this indoctrination shall carry on and will become self re-fueling and self-generating for hundreds of years, maybe thousands. Don't forget you must pitch the old Black males, the young Black male, and the young Black male against the old Black male. You must use the dark skin slaves vs. the light skin slaves and light skin slaves vs. the dark skin slaves. You most use the female vs. the male, and the male vs. the female. You must also have "our white servants and overseers distrust all Blacks, but are necessary that your slaves trust and depend on us. They must love, respect and trust only us. Gentlemen, these kits are your keys to control. Use them. Have your wives and children use them, never miss an opportunity. If used intensely for one year, the slaves themselves will remain perpetually distrustful. Thank you, gentlemen:[117]

The above strategies shared by Willie Lynch with the American slave owners had a very devastating effect on the, African American families. It destroyed the structure of the family and emasculated the men of their masculinity and ability to contribute to the stability of their families and community. The residual effects of the Willie Lynch strategies are evidenced in our community even to this day. Pharaoh, the Egyptian rulers, used a similar genocidal strategy during the history of the Israelites. Pharaoh gave orders to his officials that "all male boys should be destroyed upon birth by the midwives (Exodus 1:16)." He knew that if the boys were killed, then the race would cease to exist. Much damage is done by systems in America to African American youth. To those who

---

[117] http://www.finalcall.com/artman/publish/Perspectives_1/Willie_Lynch_letter_The_Making_of_a_Slave.shtml

are not killed by violence, in jail, unemployed or underemployed, the remainder of African American men fair statistically lower than whites and a growing number of Hispanics.

The goal for developing a manual for men mentoring men is to protect African American men by equipping them with godly guidelines and lifestyles that overcomes systems that work contrary to this objective. Godly men in the Bible are also promised long life and prosperity when they obey God and live according to His Word.[118]

Theologically, this project is supported by the presupposition that it requires a man to mentor a man. "As iron sharpens iron, so one man sharpens another"[119] Looking beyond the notions of maleness, a man becomes a productive man because there were and are men in their lives.

> And God said, Let the earth bring forth grass, the herb yielding seed, and the fruit tree yielding fruit after his kind, whose seed is in itself, upon the earth: and it was so.[120]

This text presupposes a principle of reproduction that guides the development of the manual.

The phenomenon of the African American male to be addressed in this project is understood sociologically as well, in an anthology of the black family, June and Parker draw on various writers regarding the residual effects of slavery, systemic racism and oppression.[121] The authors further support the significance of this project by the ways African Americans have been misunderstood in their plight to overcome the residual and ongoing effects of the experience of slavery in America.

---

[118]   Psalm 1
[119]   Proverbs 27:17
[120]   Genesis 1:11
[121]   Lee N. June and Matthew Parker, eds., The Black Family (Grand Rapids: Zondervan Publishing House, 1991).

Casual observers often assume that Blacks have had social experiences that closely resemble those of their own ethnic group. To illustrate, other ethnic and racial groups will often say that their ancestors overcame prejudice, discrimination, poverty, and oppression-so why cannot Blacks do the same? This type of thinking ignores pertinent sociological evidence (Feagin, 1984). The sociological experiences of Black Americans are not comparable to those of any other ethnic group in the United States, despite social science prognostications to the contrary (Lieberson, 1980).[122]

To argue for the particularity of this project's focus on African American men and not all men, June and Parker, continues:

Blacks alone have experienced the irreparable complications of attempted genetic genocide, of being uprooted from their ancestral families and simultaneously deprived of names, culture, legacy, inheritance, and sponsorship from the old country. Blacks alone have survived the vicious dehumanization of slavery across generations, only to find themselves ushered into segregation and economic dependency by a society unwilling to make appropriate restitution for its atrocities against them. Blacks alone have watched as their labor, creativity, and productivity has been exploited from generation to generation. No other ethnic group has come close to; this pariah status (Omi and Winant, 1986).[123]

In addition, African Americans have also experienced a division in their families by the social agencies in our urban cities. It was a matter of policy for the agencies to demand that the husband

---

[122]   Ibid, 18.
[123]   Ibid, 18.

or father of children in a family who rely on assistance, to be removed from the home.

A violation of this policy could result in the families being expelled from the assistance program. There are many problems facing African American families in America. This project will focus on two of those problems impacting the men in the Bethany Baptist Church and its Westside Community.

Matthew Parker raises some social science questions and offers ministerial support and solutions to address some of the problems faced by men in the African American families the African American Man and Lane's discussion four basic needs:

> "...family, a life mission, a social context that affirms his significance, and a relationship with God through Jesus Christ...
>
> Admittedly, we must first make sure that they come and that they are sufficiently attracted to our churches, organizations, and programs, to make the effort to participate.
>
> For older men, it's late in the game and their habits are set. The best way to reach African American male adults is by one-on-one interaction. Men will not always respond to even the most fervent appeals beat the pulpit. Men who are connected to Jesus Christ and to a local church family must make the effort to evangelize other men on their jobs and in their neighborhoods. The best way for them to do that is through "relationship evangelism". As men, we have to make the effort to form friendships and relationships that go past the superficial level and put us in a position to be open with other men about our challenges and struggles and to show and demonstrate how we have overcome them through our spiritual

relationship and by following the wisdom outlined in the Word of God.[124]

There is both a passion and urgency at work in the development of this project. The power of the gospel for impacting individuals provides great promise the local church, families and communities. The project is a direct challenge to "the acceptable year," declared by the Lord in the poignant text.

> The Spirit of the Lord is upon me, because he bath anointed me to preach the gospel to the poor: he hath sent me to heal the brokenhearted, to preach deliverance to the captives, and recovery of sight to the blind, to set at liberty them that are bruised, To preach the acceptable year of the Lord.[125]

This project, therefore, seeks to develop a manual that results in mentored men who are transformed, [126] conformed,[127] and represent the new creation.[128] African American men, who after being mentored by other African American men, will become leaders in the local church, strengthen their families, and he agents of change in the community.

Context:

The Bethany Baptist Church of Detroit is located on the Westside of Detroit in a predominantly African American community. There are more than 300 members on the church roll, but only about 150 members attend on a regular basis. The ratio of women to men is four to one. The focus of this project will be the

---

[124] Matthew, Parker Teaching Our Men Reaching Our Fathers (Detroit: Matthew Parker, 2000), 40.
[125] Luke 4:18–19.
[126] Romans 12:1,2.
[127] Romans 8:29
[128] 2 Corinthians 5:17; Galatians 4:19.

development of a "men-to-men" mentoring manual as a means of increasing the attendance and active participation of men in the church.

As one walks through the community of the Bethany Baptist Church, one would find many homes headed by females with a high school education or less; According to the 2000 census, these families generally living at the lowest level of poverty with minimum provisions for their children and themselves. The neighborhood is generally low-income and made up of a low socio-economic population. Consequently, the crime rate is generally high, the education rate is low, and jobless rates are high. It is obvious to see that the odds are against children in this community to succeed in the larger culture.

The homes are mostly modest sized bungalows that are usually rented by the families. A casual drive through the area would remind someone of a war zone. Many of the homes have been gutted or demolished. What was once a thriving community of persons owning and maintaining their homes has become a haven of neglect which are occupied by the near homeless and destitute, who are renters. The property value in this area is significantly lower than those homes in nearby communities.

It is in this kind of environment from which some of the young men come to the Bethany Baptist Church. Usually, the boys in these families do not have men as role models. These young boys often find negative male role models in the gangs of their community. It is imperative for the church to reach out to these young men in the church and its community with divine intervention and resources. If the church does not accept this responsibility, no other entity or institution will.

This project is significant because it seeks to address two problems that exist in the context of low male attendance and participation in the church. The approach used is in-reach and outreach ministry to men. Using a "men mentoring men" concept drawn flow Scripture[129] this manual seeks to both increase the number of men active in church and men who will serve as mentors to the men within and without the church.

There are many differences between the men in the congregation and those living in the community. The average member of the Bethany Baptist Church has a high school diploma. Some of the younger members have college degrees, professional degrees, and trade professions. Overall, the membership of Bethany Baptist Church could be classified as middle class. The majority of the African American people living in the church community are low-income families. Many of the homes have single or divorced mothers as the head of households. Many of the members in this community are unemployed, underemployed, or living off of government subsidies. According to the 2000 census, many of the people living in the 48228 zip code have less than a high school education,

The Westside community where Bethany Baptist Church is located will be reached by lay-men who will assume the responsibility for mentoring their peers. Traditionally, the pastor fulfills this responsibility. Research indicates the value of peer relationships toward achieving the goal of increasing the number of men who attend church. Increasing the attendance of males to the active membership of the church has far reaching implications for strengthening families' life in the community, and the stability of the congregation.

The New Testament Church, notwithstanding its patriarch at culture, establishes a paradigm for a manual for men mentoring men. This project particularly focuses on men and is not intended to value men over women. The local congregation supports an egalitarian position between men and women. However, men are disproportionately represented in the congregation. An increase of men in the congregation will not limit or restrict opportunities

---

[129]   Proverbs 27:17 and 2 Timothy 2:2

for women. This effort would enhance the ministry for both men and women as they do ministry.

The developments of churches in the New Testament provide a theological basis for developing a "men mentoring men" manual that addresses the relational deficit that exists between men. The depth of mentoring indicated in the text that says, "and the things which you have heard from me in the presence of many witnesses, these entrust to faithful men, who will be able to teach others also," will form the development of the manual. [130] Essentially, men will be mentored in a way that they in turn will mentor others. It provides for a strategy that results in the ongoing evangelization of men. When the writer to the Galatians says "Bear one another's burdens, and thus fulfill the law of Christ," [131] the notion of relationship becomes the focus. The manual provides for men in community to share intimacy and vulnerability through learning interpersonal skills.

This writer serves the context as Associate Regional Minister for American Baptist Churches. Assuming the similarity of this context with other urban congregations, there is a high probability for replication. The writer is called upon to provide consultation to pastors and lay leaders. This manual promises to become a valuable resource.

Significant Terms:

Mentoring – is a ministry of impartation. Crosby defines mentoring as "a brain to pick, a shoulder to cry on, and a kick in the pants."[132] For this project mentoring is akin to the presupposition drawn from The Lathan writer which says, "A pupil is not above his teacher; but everyone, after he has been fully trained, will

---

[130] 2 Timothy 2:2
[131] Galatians 6:2
[132] John C. Crosby as quoted in Robert Vann's Principles for effective Mentoring, Washington, D.C.: 1998, 26.

be like his teacher."[133] Mentoring is discipling with the teacher having boldness of courage to say, "be."

Mentoree – A man who is mentored by another man who has been trained. The mentor is able to guide the mentoree with biblical principles, and to establish a loving relationship as a Christian brother.

Evangelism – for this project is limited to the outreach that occurs through mentoring. It is expected that at times the process of mentoring may be initiated in a nontraditional setting that is outside of the church. The classical modalities for evangelism will not be discussed. It is anticipated that a form of evangelism will result when men focus on relationship building instead of proselytizing.

Discipleship – In this context, this term refers to the process of mentoring men within the Bethany Baptist Church and its Westside community.

Active Participation – the men in the church functioning in leadership positions and attending on a regular basis. The men also are engaging one another and younger males in the congregation, providing role modeling and support.

Project Goals:

This project seeks to impact the status of the men in the Bethany Baptist Church and its Westside Community by increasing the attendance and participation of men through a mentoring training process. The men will begin to take leadership roles in the church so that they can become mentors to young males growing up in homes that are headed by females. Their balance in

---

[133] Luke 6:40

the leadership of the church as a result of greater male attendance and participation. Some of the specific goals that will be learned by the men from the mentoring training are:

- Men will become students of the Bible.
- Men will learn the importance of being in relationship with others.
- Men will have an increase understanding of their role as spiritual leaders.
- Men will understand the importance of integrity, honesty, and morality.

Personal goals for this project are:

- To increase my understanding of mentoring.
- To train others how to mentor.
- To recognize those who have mentors.
- To recognize those who are my mentors.
- To increase my awareness of what it means to mentor others.

Design and Procedure:

The development of this model will proceed in three phases. First, random surveys of African American pastors (see appendixes) will be conducted. The survey solicits general responses from urban African American pastors regarding their opinions about ministries to African American men. More particularly, the survey addresses concerns about ministries that focus on African American men. Pastors that were identified as having successful men ministries were sought out to determine "what they were doing." Data from these pastors along with information gleaned from a review of the literature will be the basis upon which the mentoring project will be developed.

The second phase of the project involves a survey of African American men both orally and written. Primarily, this survey is given to ascertain the needs of African American men and how they feel about the church, pastors, leadership, and power. Data gleaned from this survey will be integrated with phase one data to further develop the project manual.

The third phase is the development of the "men-to-men" mentoring manual. The manual will consist of lessons that will he taught over twenty-five weeks. Participants will be limited to twenty men from the congregation. These classes will help to shape the manual which when full developed, will be evaluated by a cross selection of experts. A survey of the men participating in the classes will be conducted to determine their reflections on personal growth. The writer serves as the initial mentor to the twenty participants [or mentorees]. The experts will be the evaluators.

The fourth phase will consist of an evaluation of the manual by pastors of African American men. Those pastors and authors who have demonstrated expertise in the areas of ministering to African American men will be selected as evaluators. Some of these pastors will be identified from phase one activity. Other pastors will be identified later in the project to participate in the evaluation. Additionally, non-pastors, some of whom are authors and researchers, will be sought for their expert evaluation. The manual evaluated will be labeled Manual (Draft), the manual developed after the evaluation will be labeled Manual (Revised).

The value of this method for developing the manual will be its adaptability in varied urban settings. The results from the impact of the lessons taught in the projects context balanced with the results from experts encourages the development of a user-friendly manual.

Assessment:

The first goal of the project is to increase the attendance of men in the Bethany Baptist Church through mentoring training. There will be a count of the number of men attending church before the training, and another count of the men after the training to determine if there was an increase in attendance.

The second goal of the project is to determine the degree of active participation in the church by its men members. A survey will be given to the men to determine their activities in the church before the training, and another survey given, after the training to determine if the degree of activity by the men increased in the church.

Calendar:

Prospective Dates

Project approval
Survey One
Manual lessons developed
Training Classes held
First Draft
Second Draft
Final Draft
Defense

Core Team

Ned Adams Jr., D.Min., Advisor
Professor of Pastoral Counseling; Director of Pastoral Counseling
Ashland Theological Seminary

Samuel Bullock Jr., D.Min., Field Consultant
Pastor of Bethany Baptist Church; First Vice President of Council of Baptist Pastors of Detroit and Vicinity; Officer on the Board of MOSES (Metropolitan Strategic Enabling Strength)

Kenneth Harris, Resource, D.Min., Consultant
Pastor of Baptist Temple Church, Associate Professor, Ecumenical Theological Seminary; Adjunct Professor, Ashland Theological Seminary; Chair of Education Committee, Council of Baptist Pastors of Detroit and Vicinity

Matthew Parker, D.Min., Resource Consultant and author
President of the Institute for Black Family Development in Detroit, Michigan

Support Team:

Ida Stevenson, MS in counseling, the wife of the writer who is also a master teacher.
Harold Gunn, Ph.D., a psychologist, who is a friend of the writer.
George Vaughn, D.Min., who is a friend and colleague of the writer who serves on the staff of a local church.

Appendix Seven

Please answer the following questions related to the mentoring training you received in the church.

Disagree Strongly			Disagree Somewhat		Agree		Strongly Agree		
1	2	3	4	5	6	7	8	9	10

I.)   The mentoring training you received was effective.

Disagree Strongly			Disagree Somewhat		Agree		Strongly Agree		
1	2	3	4	5	6	7	8	9	10

II.)   Your attendance in church has improved after mentoring training.

Disagree Strongly			Disagree Somewhat		Agree		Strongly Agree		
1	2	3	4	5	6	7	8	9	10

III.)   Your role in the family has improved since mentoring training.

Disagree Strongly			Disagree Somewhat		Agree		Strongly Agree		
1	2	3	4	5	6	7	8	9	10

IV.)   Your leadership role in the church and community has improved since mentoring training.

Disagree Strongly			Disagree Somewhat		Agree		Strongly Agree		
1	2	3	4	5	6	7	8	9	10

V.)   You were active in church prior to mentoring training.

Disagree Strongly			Disagree Somewhat		Agree		Strongly Agree		
1	2	3	4	5	6	7	8	9	10

VI.)   Your church activities increased after mentoring training.

Disagree Strongly			Disagree Somewhat		Agree		Strongly Agree		
1	2	3	4	5	6	7	8	9	10

VII.)   Your trust for the church increased after the mentoring training.

Disagree Strongly			Disagree Somewhat		Agree		Strongly Agree		
1	2	3	4	5	6	7	8	9	10

VIII.) Your trust for the pastor has increased after mentoring training.

Disagree Strongly   Disagree Somewhat   Agree   Strongly Agree

1   2   3   4   5   6   7   8   9   10

IX.) The quality of your relationship with other men has improved.

Disagree Strongly   Disagree Somewhat   Agree   Strongly Agree

1   2   3   4   5   6   7   8   9   10

X.) Your relationship with God has improved after the mentoring training

Disagree Strongly   Disagree Somewhat   Agree   Strongly Agree

1   2   3   4   5   6   7   8   9   10

XI.) Your role as a mentoree was rewarding.

Disagree Strongly   Disagree Somewhat   Agree   Strongly Agree

1   2   3   4   5   6   7   8   9   10

The Epilogue

This book represents a journey that began in Birmingham, Alabama where I was born into a family of working class parents who instilled in my sister, Judy and me a desire to get an education and live up to our fullest potential. It was also a community that offered us hope in the schools we attended and the church where we first learned about God.

It is the God of my father and ancestors, the liberator, and emancipator who led us to Detroit, Michigan for jobs and higher education. My hope for those who read this manual and those who will benefit from its implementation will also strive to reach their full potential in this land of opportunities. The election of Barack Hussein Obama as president of the United States of America has inspired me and may others to know that "yes we can."

I still share the dream with Dr. Martin Luther King, Jr. stating that we look forward to the day when we will not be judged by the pigmentation of our skin, but by the content of our character among fellow Americans.

However, it appears that in spite of the closeness of the dream, we are still experiencing "nightmares of incidences" when we consider the outcome of the "Trayvon Martin" murder case in which the defendant was found not guilty by an all female and mostly white jury. For that reason and others, I consider this manual to be an essential tool preparing African American males to survive in a hostile, deadly and threatening environment in many of the communities across America.

Selected Bibliography

Abatso, George, and Yvonne Abatso. *How to Equip the African American Family.* Chicago: Urban Ministries, 1991.

Bey, Theresa M, and Thomas C. Holmes. *Mentoring: Developing Successful New Teachers.* Reston: Association of Teacher Educators, 1990.

Boyd, Stephen B. *The Men We long to Be.* San Francisco: Harper, 1995.

Cavanagh, John R. *Fundamental Pastoral Counseling.* Milwaukee: The Bruce Publishing Company, 1962.

Cobb, Jr., John B. *Theology and Mentoring.* Philadelphia: Fortress Press, 1977.

Cone, James H, and Wilmore S Gayraud. *Black Theology a Documentary History Volume One.* New York: Orbis Books, 1993.

Crabb, Larry. *Men & Women.* Grand Rapids: Zondervan Publishing, 1993.

Dicks, Russell I. *Principles and Practices of Mentoring.* Englewood Cliffs: Prentice-Hall, 1963.

Fisher, Biddy. *Mentoring.* London: Library Association, 1994.

Gerkin, Charles V. *An Introduction to Mentoring.* Nashville: Abingdon Press, 1997.

Godwin, Andre. *The Pastor Counselor.* New York: Holt, Rinehart and Winston, 1965.

Green, Bernard D. *Couseling and Advice Giving in Mentoring.* Iowa: Wm. C. Brown, 1987.

Hicks, Robert. *The Masculine Journey.* Colorado: Navpress, 1993.

Hiltener, Seward. *Preface of Pastoral Theology.* Nashville: Abington, 1958.

Hull, Bill. *The Disciple Making Pastor.* Old Tappan: Revell, 1988.

Hulme, William E. *The Mentoring of Families.* New York: Abingdon Press, 1962.

June, Lee N, and Matthew Parker. *Men to Men*. Grand Rapids: Zondervan, 1996.

Klaver, Dick Brian. *Men at Peace*. Nashville: Thomas Nelson, 1993.

Kunjufu, Jawanza. *Adam Where Are You? Why Most Black Men Don't Go to Church*. Nashville: Copywritten Material, 1994.

Lee, Courtland C. "Saving the Native Son: Empowering Strategies for Young Black Men." *Eric Document*, 1996: 1-102.

Macon, Larry L. *Discipling The African American Men*. Winston-Derek Publishing, 1997.

Maxwell, John C. *Developing The Leader Within You*. Nashville: Thomas Nelson, 1993.

Mays, Benjamin E. *Born to Rebel*. Athens: The University of Georgia Press, 1971.

McIntyre, Donald, Margaret Wilkin, and Hazel Hagger. *Mentoring: Perspectives on School-Based Teacher Education*. Philadelphia: Kogan page, 1993.

Mincy, Ronald B. *Nurturing Young Black Men*. Lanham: National Book, 1994.

Mink, Oscar G, Keith Q Owen, and Barbara P Mink. *Developing High-Performance People The Art of Coaching*. Reading: Addison-Wesley, 1993.

Mullen, Carol A. *Breaking the Circle of One*. New York: Lang, 1997.

Murray, Margo, and Marna A Owen. *Beyond The Myths and Magic of Mentoring*. San Francisco: Jossey-Bass, 1991.

Nance, Terry. *God's Armor Bearer, Book II*. Tulsa: Harrison House, 1972.

Nix, Sheldon D. *Becoming Effective Fathers and Mentors*. Colorado: Cook, 1996.

Oglesby, Jr., William B. *Biblical Themes for Mentoring*. Nashville: Abingdon, 1980.

Oliver, Gary J. *Real Men Have Feelings Too*. Chicago: Moody Press, 1993.

Otes, Wayne E. *Protestant Pastoral Counseling*. Philadelphia: The Westminister Press, 1962.

Parker, Matthew. *The African American Church: How to Start A Men's Health Project*. Detroit: Family Resources, 1997.

Sample, Tex. *Ministry in an Oral Culture-Living Will Rogers, Uncle Remus and Minnie Pearl*. Louisville: Westminister/John Knox Press, 1994.

Schachter-Shalomi, Zalman. *From Ageing to Sageing*. New York: Warner Books, 1995.

Schlessinger, Laura. *Ten Stupid Things Men do to Mess up Their Lives*. New York: Cliff Street Books, 1997.

Timothy, Operation. "Christian Business Men's Committe." Chattanooga, 1955.

Torrey, R. A. *how to bring men to CHRIST*. Springdale: Whitaker House, 1984.

Vanderpool, James A. *Person To Person*. Garden City: Doubleday, 1997.

Vann, Robert. *Principles for Effective Mentoring to Ex-Prisioners*. Washington: Prison Fellowship, 2000.

Walker, Clarence. *Biblical Counseling with African Americans*. Grand Rapids: Zondervan, 1992.

Wilmore, Gayraud. *Black Men in Prison*. Atlanta: ITC Press, 1990.

Yeomans, Robin, John Sampson, and ed. *Mentorship in the Primary School*. Washington: The Falmer Press, 1994.

This manual explores the history and the potential of African American men in the Black Church as agents of change in to contribute to strengthening the church, families and communities.

Consistently, across urban communities in the United States, this phenomenon of low numbers of African American men, who actively participate and attend church in relation to that of African American women, is the norm.

It shows the need to strengthen churches, families and communities. African American pastors suggest this correlated with increasing participation and attendance of African American men in the ministries of the local church.